GEMS *of* THOUGHT
for
FRATERNAL SPEAKERS
in
POETRY *and* PROSE

Gems of Thought

FOR FRATERNAL SPEAKERS

IN POETRY AND PROSE

REVISED AND ENLARGED

 *With Special Addresses*

for Officers of the Order of the Eastern Star

for Important Occasions in the Chapter Year

COMPILED BY E. B. RIEGEL

Including CEREMONIES

BY VARIOUS AUTHORS

RICHMOND, VIRGINIA
MACOY PUBLISHING AND MASONIC
SUPPLY COMPANY, INC.

Printed in the United States of America

CONTENTS

v

FOREWORD

MANY inquiries for a collection of pertinent and pithy selections suitable for fraternal addresses are responsible for the publication of this volume. Each season brought its quota of requests for something that could be used for the regular fraternal occasions, and these were interspersed with requests for addresses appropriate for unusual events.

Long association and a thorough familiarity with the needs of fraternal officers on the part of the compiler made it possible to select and prepare the required material. Much time and thought were spent in procuring the selections in this volume, particular care being taken to avoid the hackneyed and stereotyped expressions which are distasteful to speaker and audience alike.

Not only are the selections usable as they stand, but for many they contain the germ of an idea which will enable officers to clothe the thought in words of their own. This gives the book a still wider range of usefulness.

Much as we should have liked to give full credit wherever possible, it has been difficult to ascertain the sources of many verses and prose selections taken from Proceedings and various publications. Should offense be given unwittingly to any author who has been quoted without appropriate credit, we shall gladly make amends by an acknowledgment line in our next edition.

THE PUBLISHERS.

1. WORDS OF WELCOME

You are welcome as the sunshine
That drives the clouds away;
You are welcome as the restful night
That ends the restless day.

You are welcome as the dewdrops
That kiss the flowers to life;
You are welcome as the kindly words
That end a bitter strife.

Take all the loving greetings
That memory's halls will lend
And they are but half the welcome
We here to you extend.

We would like to make you happy,
And we want to bring you cheer;
Just to keep you smiling merrily
Every moment you are here.

So, just as a beginning,
We are greeting you this way;
With many, many happy thoughts
To bring you joy today.

☆   ☆   ☆   ☆   ☆

WELCOME is a happy word,
It makes the heart with gladness sing;
And like the sweet voice of a bird,
Through long hours its echoes ring.

☆　☆　☆　☆　☆

IT only takes a little love
To make a life more sweet;
It only takes a little cheer
To make a day complete.

It only takes a little smile
To brighten our pathway;
So here's a little bit of both
To welcome you today.

☆　☆　☆　☆　☆

PAST Matrons and Past Patrons, too,
We give you hearty cheer;
And may you long be spared to meet
With those assembled here.

Your labors long and earnest
We fain would well requite;
And make you feel thrice welcome
In your Chapter Room tonight.

☆　☆　☆　☆　☆

TAKE all the loving greetings
That memory's halls will lend
And they are but half the welcome
We here to you extend.

☆　☆　☆　☆　☆

THE word "welcome" contains seven important letters, and each letter stands for a friendly thought—

WELCOME

W　stands for the *warmth* of our hearts
E　tells how *eagerly* we do our part
L　is the *love* we hold for you
C　stands for *comradeship,* loyal and true
O　is the *Order* to which we all belong
M　for the *members,* so steady and strong
E　is for *everything else* we would say

In the very glad "welcome" we give you today.

☆　☆　☆　☆　☆

THERE'S a deep sort of joy that we all understand,
In the ring of a voice and the clasp of a hand;
In the warmth of a smile that is friendly and true.
This greeting, my friends, is extended to you.

☆　☆　☆　☆　☆

THE simple word "welcome" cannot express all that is in our hearts today, but it is the one word in our language which is oftenest used to voice gladness and joy at one's coming.

3

May you find the true spirit of hospitality in our midst and may you take with you the memory of inspiring friendship and fraternal fellowship.

☆　　☆　　☆　　☆　　☆

THE word "welcome" is like the "old story of love." It never grows old, but is sweeter with each repetition.

☆　　☆　　☆　　☆　　☆

WE especially welcome to our hearthstone those who are with us for the first time. May you be impressed with the spirit of fraternalism and may you say in your hearts, "it was good to be in their midst."

☆　　☆　　☆　　☆　　☆

MAY joy and peace and love attend you here and may your visit bring such a vision of our glorious Star in the East that you will radiate added light and inspiration, wherever you may be. Again we greet you.

☆　　☆　　☆　　☆　　☆

THE Three Wise Men, meeting on the desert plain, were drawn together by their common purpose. They welcomed each other as fellow travelers on the same road, moving to the same destination, with the Star of Bethlehem guiding them. So we welcome you.

☆　　☆　　☆　　☆　　☆

WELCOME! What a wealth of meaning the word possesses; what magic warmth it holds. It makes us forget the word "stranger" and causes us to remember that we are all members of one large family—the fraternal fam-

4

ily—banded together for a great purpose, the fellowship of mankind.

☆   ☆   ☆   ☆   ☆

DEAR SISTER, anything I might say to welcome you, the most eloquent words in the gift of human tongues, would seem poor and inadequate to express the love and admiration we have in our hearts for you, who have labored so long and so faithfully for the good of our Order. This meeting would not be complete without your presence.

☆   ☆   ☆   ☆   ☆

I DO trust you will enjoy every minute of your stay with us, and when this meeting is ended may you carry home with you memories that time can never erase, blessings for you in your year's work, unforgettable friendships, loving kindnesses that can bring honey from a rock and sweet waters from the barest desert, the faith, hope, charity and love that right all wrongs. May you have beautiful memories, sweet and tender, that will linger like the perfume of roses in your heart of hearts.

☆   ☆   ☆   ☆   ☆

I WISH you could know fully what a pleasure it has been to prepare for your coming and how eagerly we have looked forward to the time when we could meet, mingle fraternally and work together for the one great cause of our beloved Order and to strengthen the fra-

5

ternal chain of fellowship which makes us one big family.

☆　　☆　　☆　　☆　　☆

In welcoming you with all the warmth of our hearts, we are inspired by friendship for each other and devotion to the principles we all represent. Here the opportunity is offered to renew and strengthen our allegiance at the altar of our Chapter, extending love and honor to all who have looked through the darkness upon the radiance of the Star of the East.

☆　　☆　　☆　　☆　　☆

We welcome you to our city, we welcome you to our councils, and we welcome you to our hearts. You are thrice welcome, nay, a hundred times you are welcome and we are fortunate in having this opportunity to renew the ties of fellowship that strengthen through the passing years and to enrich our lives with new friendships.

☆　　☆　　☆　　☆　　☆

To our distinguished guests—I am pleased to add my personal greetings to the warm words of welcome already expressed. I heartily welcome you and trust that as we are privileged to commune together we may all improve the opportunity to cultivate and strengthen the fraternal bonds which are the greatest forces in human friendships.

May the absent ones be conscious of the loving thoughts which we are silently sending to them.

☆　　☆　　☆　　☆　　☆

THE gates of the city are open to you; the doors of the Temple swing inward for you; our hearts invite you to enter.

☆　☆　☆　☆　☆

THE word "welcome" is the keynote of all hospitality. It opens the doors of our hearts and draws forth friendly greetings and sincere handclasps.

In this spirit we greet you today and we hope your stay in our midst will be very happy and always remain a treasured memory.

☆　☆　☆　☆　☆

AND now, sisters and brothers, we receive you as our guests and bid you a most royal welcome. What is ours we gladly make yours. We want you to be very happy during your sojourn among us. We appreciate the effort you have made to be here and we are honored to have you as our guests.

☆　☆　☆　☆　☆

WELCOME TO THE DISTRICT DEPUTY

By DOROTHY TRIMBLE, P.M. (*Indiana*)

Always welcome as can be
Is a District Deputy,
She briefs us with her little notes
As sign and rules and passes she quotes
Because her purpose is to see
That we perform efficiently.

Now, we, too, have a little book,
And in it, as we take a look,
Our findings are, to all intent,
She rates with us, 100%.

As a business man has an office girl,
And a housewife, a deep-freeze,
So a Worthy Grand Matron has deputies
To do her work with ease,
From all parts of our home state,
Dark, fair, or short, or tall,
Come our marvelous district deputies,
Sure enough, we love them all.

☆　　☆　　☆　　☆　　☆

2. RESPONSES TO WORDS OF WELCOME

It's a grand and glorious feeling
When we hear such cordial cheer,
And to know that someone wants us
When they say, "I'm glad you're here."

There's a thrill in hearty greetings
That the soul delights to feel,
And there's joy in loving welcome
From the friends we know are real.

☆ ☆ ☆ ☆ ☆

Few pleasures in life are so fine and so sweet
As this welcome of yours; it is gracious, complete.
Our hearts' full response tells how happy we are
To meet here together, as Star with Star.

☆ ☆ ☆ ☆ ☆

You have given us a welcome
Most hearty and sincere;
Just to hear your Matron's address
Makes us glad that we are here.

☆ ☆ ☆ ☆ ☆

In the journey through the labyrinth of life, there is nothing that brings a deeper thrill than a warm, sincere welcome. You have indeed made our coming among you seem truly royal.

☆ ☆ ☆ ☆ ☆

9

My joy and happiness in the privilege of meeting with you is so much greater than I can find words to express. I have looked forward with keen anticipation to this moment and my fondest hopes have been realized from the moment I entered your Chapter room. The warmth of your welcome will be one of my happiest memories. Your generous hospitality is exceedingly dear to me and I shall be loathe to leave you. I thank you for courtesies extended me while in your midst.

☆   ☆   ☆   ☆   ☆

THIS warmest of welcomes brings a surge of happiness welling up in my heart, a sense of being cherished and loved. It is in your smiles, in your hearty handclasps, and in your expressions of affection and good wishes.

☆   ☆   ☆   ☆   ☆

VISITS always give pleasure—if not the arrival, the departure. —PORTUGUESE PROVERB.

☆   ☆   ☆   ☆   ☆

3. GOOD WISHES TO INCOMING WORTHY MATRON OR WORTHY PATRON

God be with you, when breaks the early dawn
And sunlight floods the scene with glorious gold;
And may He bless you as each day is born
With every happiness your heart can hold.

God be with you at noon, when the sun is high
And all around is bathed in warmth and light;
When life is glad and loving friends are nigh,
May He uphold and keep you ever in His sight.

God be with you, when falls the twilight gray,
The sun goes down and evening time draws near;
May peaceful moments at the close of day
Bring tender memories of all your heart holds dear.

God be with you, through all the silent night
When in the firmament bright stars shall shine;
And while in dreams your fancy takes its flight
God hold you ever with His love divine.

☆　☆　☆　☆　☆

The sweetest music ever heard,
The sweetest perfume ever stirred,
Cannot compare with these dear words,
The simple wish: "God bless you."

☆　☆　☆　☆　☆

I SHOULD like to send you a sunbeam,
The twinkle of some bright star;
Or a tiny piece, of the downy fleece,
That clings to a cloud afar.

I should like to send you the dewdrops,
That sparkle at break of day;
And then, at night, the eerie light,
That mantles the Milky Way.

I should like to send you the power,
That nothing can overthrow;
The power to laugh and to smile, the while
A-journeying through life you go.

But these are mere fanciful wishes,
I'll send you Godspeed instead;
I'll clasp your hand, then you'll understand,
All the things I have left unsaid.

☆　☆　☆　☆　☆

MAY the dreams you have dreamed in the waiting years,
When hope in your heart was high;
Those strange, sweet dreams which nobody knew,
Of the wonderful things you had hoped to do,
Come true as the year goes by.

May the flame that burned in the heart of your dreams,
Like the flame on the hearth of home;
In your life remain, as a living sign,

GOOD WISHES TO INCOMING MATRON

Of human faith and love divine,
In this year that is to come.

☆　☆　☆　☆　☆

I HOPE that as your path of life
Goes winding through the years,
'Twill lead through fields of happiness
Avoiding vales of tears;
With many a pleasant resting place
From stress of work and play,
And many a friendly comrade's face
To smile a greeting on your way.

☆　☆　☆　☆　☆

GOD's hand to guard you tenderly, whate'er betide,
His light within your soul, to be a daily guide,
His benediction fair, to rest upon your life;
His joy so full, His grace so blest, to calm all strife,
His love so tender and so true, to bless your way.
This is my heartfelt wish for you along your way.

☆　☆　☆　☆　☆

YOU'VE a little way about you that is very, very dear;
A pleasant way, that always makes one glad to have you
near.
That brings a smile to welcome you, a sigh when you
depart;
And that little way about you has endeared you to our
hearts.

☆　☆　☆　☆　☆

13

THERE is nothing too good to wish you
But this wish I hope may come true:
That all of the sunbeams you've scattered,
Reflected, may shine back on you.

☆　☆　☆　☆　☆

MAY the Star the Wise Men followed
Guide your footsteps all the way;
May it shine in blessings on you
Every hour of every day.

☆　☆　☆　☆　☆

MAY the coming year be one of joy, of true harmony
and inspiration. May we all think and act wisely, in the
spirit of loving kindness, of co-operation and Christian
understanding. May wise counsels guide us and may all
our deliberations uphold the high standard of this
splendid Order.

☆　☆　☆　☆　☆

ADDENDUM HONORING NEWLY INSTALLED WORTHY MATRON

By FAY MAY, P.M. (*Ohio*)

*Speaking parts for A.M. and Star Points. Each S.P.
presents W.M. with a tiny shoe in appropriate color.
These may be of china, paper, or crocheted ones.*

ASSOCIATE MATRON:
　　In the year ahead, as you serve our Star,
　　You'll take many steps, near and far.

Our wishes come to you in shoes
Tinted, you'll find, in familiar hues.

ADAH:

Blue brings wishes of faithful love.
May your skies always be blue above.

RUTH:

Of patient industry all year through,
Be reminded by this yellow shoe.

ESTHER:

May you enjoy presiding each chapter night
Dressed in the color of royalty, white.

MARTHA:

With shoes of green you'll never mope.
May you find strength in faith and hope.

ELECTA:

Let red make you bright and gay,
Just as love will brighten every day.

ASSOCIATE MATRON:

May your steps be blessed the whole year through,
Then all of our wishes will come true.

☆   ☆   ☆   ☆   ☆

4. SUGGESTIONS FOR OPENING ADDRESSES OF WORTHY MATRON OR WORTHY PATRON

MY life shall touch a dozen lives
Before this year is done;
Leave countless marks for good or ill
Ere sets the evening sun.

So this the thought I always wish,
The prayer I always pray:
Lord, let my life bless other lives
It touches by the way.

☆　　☆　　☆　　☆　　☆

I SHALL need your sympathetic and understanding interest and friendship. I am counting on the same helpful support and co-operation which you have given so graciously and devotedly to my predecessors.

☆　　☆　　☆　　☆　　☆

As we stand at the threshold of a new Eastern Star year, we accept with reverence the heritage of high ideals, noble deeds, and lofty aspirations which have been handed down to us by the founders and builders of our Order.

☆　　☆　　☆　　☆　　☆

MY heart is filled to overflowing with gratitude that my sisters and brothers have advanced me, step by step,

16

until tonight you have conferred upon me the honor of the East in our Chapter.

☆ ☆ ☆ ☆ ☆

This is the day which the Lord hath made; we will rejoice and be glad in it.   —PSALM 118:24

☆ ☆ ☆ ☆ ☆

THERE are special days that stand out in everyone's life and tower above the level of ordinary events. Such a day you have given me in bestowing the leadership of our beloved Chapter for the coming year.

☆ ☆ ☆ ☆ ☆

MY symphony of life for the coming year is beautifully expressed in this little prayer: Give me the strength to keep my acts and thoughts free from malice or bitterness; help me to stand for the *hard* right against the *easy* wrong; save me from habits that harm; teach me to work as hard and play as fair in Thy sight alone as if the world saw; forgive me when I am unkind and help me to forget quickly unkindness to me; keep me ready to help others at some cost to myself; send me opportunities to do a little good every day and the insight and understanding to grasp them; and let me grow in Christlike attributes with a humble and thankful heart.

☆ ☆ ☆ ☆ ☆

TONIGHT I have experienced the joy of advancing to the highest office a Chapter accords a brother. To the

Sisters and Brothers who have chosen me as Worthy Patron, I extend my very deep appreciation.

Perhaps the most tangible way of expressing my gratitude is in constantly striving to give loyal service to my Chapter, to its members, and to the Order in general. The best of life is the joy of service and the way we serve is the test of human worth. I trust that I may come to you a year from now with a record of sincerity of purpose and action that approaches this ideal. Again, I thank you.

☆　☆　☆　☆　☆

I WANT to thank you most sincerely for the kind words you have just spoken and take this opportunity of thanking you from the bottom of my heart for the kindness and courtesy that has been shown me. I want to assure each and every one of you that I will do all that is in my power to fulfill the duties of Worthy Matron to the best of my ability. And I hope that I may perform these duties in a manner which will meet with your approval.

> The days go by and the weeks roll on
> And ere we know it the year is gone
> And now as we gather for our task
> Let wisdom be ours, is the blessing we ask

☆　☆　☆　☆　☆

5. PRESENTATIONS TO WORTHY MATRON OR WORTHY PATRON

I PRESENT to you this jewel fair,
Beautiful badge of workmanship rare;
This Star is made of purest gold,
Telling anon the sweet story of old.

Receive it and wear it and let it shine,
The sacred emblem of lessons Divine;
And should time ever the surface mar,
Brighten it with thoughts of our wonderful Star.

☆   ☆   ☆   ☆   ☆

WE wish our gift to bring to you
A chain of golden memories.
Not with links that bend and break,
For they are the kind that humans make.
But one that God has made secure,
Because it is true and good and pure.

☆   ☆   ☆   ☆   ☆

THOUGH these flowers will wither and decay,
And their perfume last for but a day;
The beauty and fragrance they now impart
Are symbols of love within each heart.
Then when these petals shall fall away
Our love will remind you of today.

☆   ☆   ☆   ☆   ☆

It is with deepest reverence that I have accepted the privilege of presenting the Chapter with this beautiful edition of the Book of Books (a gift of . . . .).

Upon our altar lies the open Bible which, despite the changes and advances of the ages, remains the greatest Modern Book—the moral manual of civilization. All through "the forest of the Psalms," through proverbs and parables, along the dreamy ways of prophecy, in gospels and epistles is heard the everlasting truth of one God who is love, and who requires of men that they love one another, do justly, be merciful, keep themselves unspotted by evil, and walk humbly before Him in whose great hand they stand. There we read of the Man of Galilee who taught that, in the far distances of the divine Fatherhood, all men were conceived in love, and so are akin—united in origin, duty, and destiny. Therefore we are to relieve the distressed, put the wanderer into his way, and divide our bread with the hungry, which is but the way of doing good to ourselves; for we are all members of one great family, and the hurt of one means the injury of all.

This profound and reverent faith from which, as from a never-failing spring, flow heroic devotedness, moral self-respect, authentic sentiments of fraternity, inflexible fidelity in life and effectual consolation in death, our Order has at all times religiously taught.

☆　☆　☆　☆　☆

Dear Sister ——————————, your progress to the East has been through our hearts, wherein your personality and character are deeply enshrined. And we present to you these flowers as the outward symbol of our sincere hope that the influence of your work will brightly glow throughout the coming years.

☆　☆　☆　☆　☆

A VERY pleasant duty has been assigned to me, an honor which I accept with genuine pleasure. It has ever been the custom of our Chapter to express in tangible form our deep feeling of appreciation and affection toward our Worthy Matron of the past year. And so, tonight, I am inexpressibly happy to present this gift on behalf of our Chapter.

Every sister and brother in the Chapter joins with me in paying you tribute. With this jewel goes our hope that it expresses to you the love and gratitude of all our hearts. We love you, and we honor you, and we will never forget your wonderful year of service to the Chapter. May everlasting joy come to you from this knowledge is our wish.

☆　☆　☆　☆　☆

(Gift to Patron)

EVER since Eve gave Adam the apple, there has been a misunderstanding between the sexes about gifts, but I sincerely hope we have selected something you will like and it comes with our love and appreciation for all you have done for our Chapter.

☆　☆　☆　☆　☆

21

IN choosing presents, people should remember that the whole point of a present is that it is "an extra."

—E. V. LUCAS.

☆　☆　☆　☆　☆

YOUR services to this Chapter warrant more than any gift we could give you. In addition to our words of thanks, we want you to have this little "extra."

☆　☆　☆　☆　☆

The Christmas spirit brings home to us—or should bring home to us—the profound Biblical truth that "it is more blessed to give than to receive." Anything which inspires unselfishness makes for our ennoblement. Christmas does that.

I am all for Christmas.　　　　　—B. C. FORBES.

☆　☆　☆　☆　☆

6. ACCEPTANCE OF JEWEL OR GIFT

DEAR SISTER _____, I am especially happy that you, with whom I have been so closely associated, should present me with this Past Matron's jewel. Ours has been a friendship of many years, one that grows sweeter and dearer with the passing of time.

☆　☆　☆　☆　☆

WITH all my heart, I appreciate this lovely gift. It speaks to me of your love through this wonderful year together. God bless each and every one of you, and thank you.

☆　☆　☆　☆　☆

"AMONG my souvenirs" are priceless gifts of gold, silver, linen, and other articles very useful and valuable. As "I count them over, every one apart" memory will recall to me the sweet and loving sentiments which accompanied them. My jar of treasured rose petals will awaken recollections of my pathway brightened with flowers.

These are all mine to claim through your generosity. But more than the material gifts, valued as they are, I appreciate the cherished thought of your efforts to make my year a success. I have sealed the remembrance of your friendship and abiding faith in my heart of hearts, to bring joy long after this wonderful year is ended.

☆　☆　☆　☆　☆

THE poet has said, "Words are the windows of the soul through which our friends view the emotions of our hearts and minds." Would that I had the eloquence to express all that is in my heart of appreciation and grateful thanks.

Throughout this wonderful year it has been my constant prayer that I might measure up in some degree to the example of those who have gone before me. I shall always appreciate the opportunity and privilege of this wonderful year.

☆   ☆   ☆   ☆   ☆

You have lavished upon me beautiful gifts, priceless gifts, priceless because of the givers and the kind thoughts that prompted the giving. My pathway has been bright with fragrant flowers, accompanied by messages of cheer and encouragement.

All of these tributes have touched the deepest well springs of sentiment within me, even though I could never find words eloquent enough to express my appreciation and enjoyment.

☆   ☆   ☆   ☆   ☆

CALVIN COOLIDGE once said, "No person was ever honored for what he received. Honor has been the reward for what he gave." I trust that in a measure I have accomplished some good in services given to the Order this past year. And I do thank you for your generosity in giving me this award.

☆   ☆   ☆   ☆   ☆

7. FAREWELL TRIBUTES TO MATRON AND PATRON

MIGHTY fine? that's only part
Of all you stand for in my heart;
Mighty genuine and square,
Mighty loyal, mighty fair.

'Twould be mighty hard to find
Many brothers half so kind;
Half so real, so good, so true,
Half so mighty nice as you.

Here's joy and peace and gladness
For the good that you have done;
For your Eastern Star devotion
And the lasting love you've won.

May the love you've given others
Follow you where'er you go;
May the lives you've cheered and cherished
Ever heartward to you flow.

☆   ☆   ☆   ☆   ☆

PATRON to each of us, Patron to all;
Kind friend, big brother, on whom we may call;
Here's luck to you, joy to you, where'er you may be,
May the Star of the East shed its radiance on thee.

☆   ☆   ☆   ☆   ☆

   I HAVE found in you a willing listener, a wise counsel-
lor and a ready sympathizer. You have given much of

your valuable time to our work and have encouraged me all of the way. I thank you for your loyalty and assistance. May blessings rich and abundant be yours.

> God bless you for the kindness
> Which you have shown to me,
> For every act of friendship
> And tender sympathy
> For all the joys you've scattered
> Along my busy way,
> Have really, truly mattered,
> Far more than I can say.

☆　☆　☆　☆　☆

MAY the very best come back to you; may your life be filled with true friends, pleasant memories, and good health; and may success serve as recompense for the devoted and able service you have given to our Chapter (or Order).

☆　☆　☆　☆　☆

IN your life, dear Worthy Matron, and in your work this year we have seen exemplified the teachings of the heroines of our Order: Fidelity to the members, Constancy to the Order, Loyalty to your officers, Faith in God and Love for one another.

☆　☆　☆　☆　☆

I TRUST this year of years will ever remain one of the brightest pages in your book of memory. As the curtain is lowered upon your splendid administration, may life bring to you in abundant measure all joy and happiness.

☆   ☆   ☆   ☆   ☆

I ESTEEM it a rare privilege to have served under the able and wise leadership of our Worthy Matron. Her ready understanding, her correct interpretation of the duties and procedure of her office, her consistent recognition of the fact that the finest results are obtained through team work—all these indicate her fitness, her abundant qualifications, for the highest station in our Chapter. She has by her charming graciousness of manner and thoughtfulness of heart endeared herself to us all. To have been her co-laborer and associate, in both official and social duties, has been to me a great pleasure, the memory of which will always remain with me.

☆   ☆   ☆   ☆   ☆

8. FAREWELLS BY WORTHY MATRON OR WORTHY PATRON

THE book of my year is before you,
Its pages more precious than gold;
And it's full of familiar faces
Of friends, both the new and the old.

There's just one regret in its passing,
Too soon has this happy year gone;
Yet faces and places enshrined there
Shall always in memory live on.

Though I have accomplished so little,
My efforts were true and sincere;
And that's why I sigh as I'm closing
The Book of My Happiest Year.

And now to my Worthy successor,
My hearty good wishes to you;
May kindness and service to others
Return richest blessings to you.

☆　☆　☆　☆　☆

WITH gratitude for the past, and an earnest prayer
for the future that God's richest blessings may ever rest
upon you, I bid you farewell.

☆　☆　☆　☆　☆

I BRING to you no message graced
With wonders I have done;

FAREWELLS BY MATRON

No great achievements can I show
At this year's set of sun.

But humbly I submit to you
The daily record of my task;
And if you please to say it's good,
'Tis all that I shall ask.

I've tried to give my best,
With heart and courage strong;
While I've prayed for keener vision
That my acts might not be wrong.

Perhaps I've erred in judgment,
Have not clearly seen the way;
Yet I'm sure you'll judge me kindly
By what I've tried to do each day.

☆   ☆   ☆   ☆   ☆

THIS is the end of a wonderful year,
The end of my journey, too;
And it leaves a thought that is deep and strong,
A wish that is kind and true.

For memory has painted this wonderful year
In colors that can never fade;
Of the happy hours I have spent with you,
Of the many friends I have made.

☆   ☆   ☆   ☆   ☆

I HAVE not tried to do wonderful things, but all the year my one thought has been to teach the principles of our Order.

☆　☆　☆　☆　☆

THE little things you said with smiling lips,
The little songs you sang, each little word,
I've stored away with loving finger tips,
Like petals of a rose the wind has stirred.
Each little kindness, your smile so gay,
These will I keep, pressed tenderly away.

And when your feet have wandered East and West,
Perhaps you will forget these little things;
Forget the old upon a newer quest.
But I will build from old rememberings,
From every word you said, with deathless art,
A towering cathedral here in my heart.

☆　☆　☆　☆　☆

MAY the Star we have followed throughout this glad year
Shine down on our pathway, bring comfort and cheer.

May the links we have added to friendship's bright chain
Grow brighter with years, and forever remain.

May the strength we have given, the hours we have
　　spent,
Reflect in our lives, bring peace and content.

May our Heavenly Father, whose love we all know,
Protect and guide us wherever we go.

☆　☆　☆　☆　☆

God bless you for the kindness which you have shown
   to me,
For every act of friendliness and tender sympathy;
For all the joys you've scattered along my pathway
   bright,
Made every task a pleasure, each meeting a delight.

☆   ☆   ☆   ☆   ☆

It has been my joy to find
At every turning of the road,
The strong arm of a comrade kind
To help me onward with my load.

And since I have no gold to give
And only love can made amends,
This is my prayer: while yet I live,
God make me worthy of my friends.

☆   ☆   ☆   ☆   ☆

Sometimes the heart cannot give forth
All that it fain would say;
Words seem but empty, useless things,
Like mists that fade away.

And so today my heart is full
Of things I can't express;
But you, who know me as you do,
Can all its meaning guess.

☆   ☆   ☆   ☆   ☆

If I have brought a little sunshine,
If I've helped to lift a care;

Made the way a little brighter,
Or a burden helped to share.

Then I'll feel that God has blessed me,
That He surely heard my prayer;
When I asked that He would lead me
And would use me everywhere.

☆ ☆ ☆ ☆ ☆

As one who cons at evening
O'er an album all alone,
And muses on the faces
Of friends that he has known;
So I turn the leaves of fancy,
'Till in shadowy design
I see in retrospection
This wondrous year of mine.

☆ ☆ ☆ ☆ ☆

THE memory of this year with you
Will linger long;
Like the sweet and tender melody
Of an old familiar song.

As the echoes of its sweetness
Sing a soft and low refrain;
And the twilight shadows gather,
I will live each scene again.

☆ ☆ ☆ ☆ ☆

AND now I have come to the end of the road
That has meant so much to me;

FAREWELLS BY MATRON

And at the end of that starlit road
I find a memory.

Of friends who have traveled along the way,
Of the spirit near and far;
That makes the fraternal bond hold sway
In our beautiful Eastern Star.

☆　☆　☆　☆　☆

YES, a year of days has slipped into eternity since you
placed in my hands the guiding of our Chapter's destiny.

☆　☆　☆　☆　☆

To Him who has kept me day by day,
To Him who has led me all the way,
To Him who has shared my every care,
To Him who has answered every prayer,
To Him who has silvered every cloud,
To Him I now would cry aloud:
　　My thanks, dear God, to Thee.

☆　☆　☆　☆　☆

I'VE tried to be a friend to those I've met from day to day
And tried to help them all I could along Life's rugged
　　way;

I've tried to say the little things that folks so like to hear,
And clasp their hands and smile, their lonely hearts to
　　cheer;

I've tried to do the little things that oft are left undone
And give the little lift by which great victories are won.

☆　☆　☆　☆　☆

33

My work is done. How well, only the Master knows;
One never sees the finish of all the seed he sows.

It may be only one's part to patiently turn the sod;
One plants, another waters, but the increase comes from
　　God.

☆　　☆　　☆　　☆　　☆

The hours I've spent with you, dear Stars,
Will ever be like pearls to me.
I'll live them over, every one apart
　　In memory.

☆　　☆　　☆　　☆　　☆

Gone are the yesterdays—folded apart,
Laid by—with treasurers I hold in my heart.

☆　　☆　　☆　　☆　　☆

God bless you, each and every one,
Best of friends beneath the sun;
Where'er I go, whate'er I do,
My heart will hold warm thoughts of you.

☆　　☆　　☆　　☆　　☆

Here is a story of the grand old time,
A tale of virtues tender, yet sublime,
Inscribed on sacred page to give us faith
In woman's constancy in life and death.
Here in God's good the bright narration see,
And five brave hearts made up the history!

Adah, great Jeptha's daughter, soul of truth;
Ruth, flower of the Moab, humble, pious Ruth;

FAREWELLS BY MATRON

Esther, the crowned, the worthiest of a crown;
Martha, His friend, whom saints and angels own;
Electa, strong the martyr's cross to bear;
These are the heroines of the Eastern Star.

Fairest among ten thousand deathless names,
How altogether lovely do they glow—
Time's annals yield no brighter, nobler themes,
No purer hearts the ranks immortal show.
Come then, oh sisters, sister virtues trace,
And light anew from them your lamps of grace.
                                    —*Rob Morris.*

☆   ☆   ☆   ☆   ☆

I DO not know where fell the seed
I've tried to sow with greatest care;
And yet I hope each seed will grow
And bring forth fruit—sometime, somewhere.

☆   ☆   ☆   ☆   ☆

I HAVE memories to treasure
All unknown a year ago;
Like sparkling gems of pleasure
Which forever I may know.

☆   ☆   ☆   ☆   ☆

I WILL pray a little prayer,
That all your years may be
Filled with days of happiness,
Like those you brought to me.

☆   ☆   ☆   ☆   ☆

If I have let into some soul a little light,
If I some pathway dark and drear have rendered bright;
If I, to one in gloom, have shown the sunny side,
Though no reward I claim, I shall be satisfied.

☆   ☆   ☆   ☆   ☆

MY successor: may her year be crowned with blessings—rich, abounding and eternal.

☆   ☆   ☆   ☆   ☆

A YEAR ago, when I first occupied the East as your
Worthy Matron, the responsibility seemed gigantic,
almost overwhelming, but strength was vouchsafed to
me in the remembrance of the love, friendship and
hearty co-operation always extended by our officers and
members. With a humble and grateful heart, I resolved
to give all that I possess—mental, physical, and spiritual.

My year's work is behind me, the record of which I
lay before you for your judgment. For my mistakes, I
ask your charitable consideration. If I have accomplished anything of lasting good, I am happy to present
it as my contribution in the service of our Order.

☆   ☆   ☆   ☆   ☆

AND tonight, as the record is brought before you and
the events of the year pass in review, I trust that for
each mistake you will plant in your heart a flower of
forgetting; for the efforts that have failed and disappointments that have come, that you will plant a
flower of understanding and encouragement; and for
the little of good that has been accomplished, I pray

that a rose of love will find a place in your garden of remembrance.

☆　☆　☆　☆　☆

SHIP ahoy! Past Worthy Matrons, and Patrons too,
For soon I'll help to steer the boat that's been steered by
　　you.

Many dangers you have faced, when the boat was small
　　and frail,
And long ago you dropped the oars, and used instead a
　　sail.

As time passed on the sailing boat, with small but fear-
　　less crew,
Became a splendid steamship, whose mast our banner
　　flew.

Keeping time with progress, the steamship passed from
　　sight,
'Til now, a powerful battleship, our Eastern Star shines
　　bright.

While sisters, holding firm the helm, steer clear from
　　every wreck,
And brothers sit in easy chairs, or lounge upon the deck.

☆　☆　☆　☆　☆

YOUR approval of my earnest endeavor will be my encouragement; the testimony of a good conscience my
support.

☆　☆　☆　☆　☆

ANOTHER link, forged from the years by which we measure time, has been added to the ever-lengthening chain which makes up the hallowed past, and is now forever a part of our Chapter's history.

☆　☆　☆　☆　☆

THE loyalty and unselfish devotion and the untiring efforts of the officers and members of our Chapter have lightened my burden, gladdened my heart, and made possible whatever success has attended my year in the East.

☆　☆　☆　☆　☆

LIKE all journeys, the road has been rough at times, there have been obstacles in my path, but loving friends have helped me on my way with deeds of kindness and expressions of their affection and confidence.

☆　☆　☆　☆　☆

YOU have stood at the gate of loyal, loving service and have inspired and cheered me on my way. Whatever of honor and of usefulness has been mine, I owe in large measure to your generous support.

☆　☆　☆　☆　☆

THE sands of time flow rapidly through the hourglass of destiny and we stand at the close of a year which has given us a wonderful opportunity to prove to others that our work means the building of a temple of service, charity and loving kindness.

☆　☆　☆　☆　☆

MAY the Star of Bethlehem, which has guided us so faithfully during the past year, continue to be our inspiration, our great Counselor and Guide, until we shall have attained the end toward which every member of the Eastern Star is striving.

☆　☆　☆　☆　☆

GRATITUDE is a memory of past blessings. Life can hold no greater treasure than the love of the friends I have made and hold through my Chapter. My thankfulness for all that our beloved Order has brought me will never cease as long as I shall live.

☆　☆　☆　☆　☆

MY greatest ambition has been to prove worthy of the trust and to discharge my duties in accordance with my appraisal of the office. I'd like to feel that I am worthy to take my place among the gentlemen who have preceded me in the office of Worthy Patron.

☆　☆　☆　☆　☆

Now comes the sunset hour at the close of the happiest year of my life. As the dawn of opportunity was ushered in with all the joy of a glorious day, so with the twilight comes the restful satisfaction of having performed this service to the best of my ability.

☆　☆　☆　☆　☆

I SHALL never cease to be grateful for the honor and privilege accorded me. I shall always recall with joy the scenes, the persons, the events, the places, and the associations which have contributed to the brightest pages in my life's volume.

☆ ☆ ☆ ☆ ☆

I ASKED of God strength, wisdom and guidance, and throughout the year I have been conscious of His never-failing help.

☆ ☆ ☆ ☆ ☆

ONLY you who have passed and traveled the "King's Highway of Service above Self" know its responsibilities, its trials, and its compensations.

☆ ☆ ☆ ☆ ☆

YOU have scattered flowers along my pathway; you have radiated love and kindness always, and memory will hold no more treasured recollections than the busy year just past.

☆ ☆ ☆ ☆ ☆

I HAVE been glad to serve my Chapter, proud to have been your Worthy Matron, and now it gives me pleasure to pass on to my successor this gavel and say, "God speed and bless you."

☆ ☆ ☆ ☆ ☆

YOU have been more than a friend, you have been the dearest of comrades; smoothing my pathway, anticipating my every wish, painting my skies a rosy hue, giving of your time and strength to help me "carry on."

☆ ☆ ☆ ☆ ☆

My association with my officers will be a picture on memory's wall that I shall recall often with pleasure and appreciation. I prize your friendship, your devotion, and your fine spirit of co-operation above everything else.

☆   ☆   ☆   ☆   ☆

To my husband, last but not least among the many blessings, is a grateful thought of love for the one who is nearer and dearer than all the world besides, whose love and devotion has made this year possible and one of the grandest years of my life. He always gave me encouragement to be brave and do my best, and if anyone deserves any praise for the work accomplished, it is he, with his wise counsel and the desire to give of the best we had to serve others.

☆   ☆   ☆   ☆   ☆

My last tribute is to one who has been my real inspiration, who has stood so faithfully by my side, guiding me with advice and counsel. He has known better than anyone else the difficulties that were mine to encounter. During the year he has been privileged to carry the distinguished title of Patron as well as husband, but in the little drama we have played he has appeared in numerous roles—chauffeur, and private secretary. For this silent service of love I shall ever be most grateful.

☆   ☆   ☆   ☆   ☆

I CANNOT close without a word of tribute, love and appreciation to one nearest and dearest to me, husband

and patron, who has stood between me and worries, who has sacrificed much to make my year a success. Never too weary to help nor too busy to accompany me, he has traveled along uncomplainingly and I am sure he will be glad that my year of short-comings and long-goings are at an end.

☆　☆　☆　☆　☆

To you, members of my official family, one and all! I wish that I might convey the full depth of my feeling for you, the keen appreciation that is mine because of your loyalty to me personally, your eagerness to work and cooperate, your perfect accord in all that might be for the advancement of the Order. Some of you have been my friends for long, whom years of association have brought especially close to my heart. Others among you have brought new and happy adventures in the realm of friendship, and tonight I feel wonderfully rich and blessed because of my association with you. What help your words of encouragement have meant to me, what joy your many expressions of love have brought me —only you can know, who also have been encouraged by friends, whose burdens have been lightened, and whose joys have been doubled because another shared them with you.

☆　☆　☆　☆　☆

In the innermost depths of my heart, I am grateful. For your never failing loyalty; for your eagerness at all times to do what seemed necessary; for your devotion to our beloved Order; for the cheerful, efficient manner in which you have performed your duties. I am grateful for this year of blessed fellowship with you and pray that the memory of our labors and pleasures together shall leave a fragrance that will linger with us always.

☆   ☆   ☆   ☆   ☆

To my Worthy Patron: I have had your always kind consideration and loyal co-operation. You are indeed eminently worthy of your official title and I shall always be grateful that the privilege of presiding in the East with you has been mine. May your future years be blessed with good health, happiness and prosperity.

☆   ☆   ☆   ☆   ☆

To my officers and committee members: A year ago I asked for your understanding co-operation and tonight I can testify that you have given it in fullest measure. Words seem feeble and meaningless when I try to express the depth of my appreciation and gratitude to you for your loyalty and helpfulness. The happy hours I have spent with you, dear friends of mine, will always remain a cherished memory.

☆   ☆   ☆   ☆   ☆

I SHALL always treasure the memory of your willing spirit of helpfulness, the confidence that has grown up between us through our close association. We believe in one another and in the years to come we will be nearer and dearer to each other. That thought is one of the great rewards for any effort I have made.

☆   ☆   ☆   ☆   ☆

43

To our Past Matrons and Past Patrons: Our beloved pioneers, who occupied the East in years past and whose wise administration of our Chapter has been a beacon light to guide me in the performance of my duties. My grateful acknowledgment to you for this fine heritage.

☆　☆　☆　☆　☆

RETIRING WORTHY MATRON'S WELCOME TO INCOMING MATRON

By Dorothy Trimble, P.M. (*Indiana*)

Each year when springtime rolls around,
We look for something new
A pretty hat, a shiny car, a Worthy Matron, too.
We always pick some special one,
And have her standing by,
Someone with loyalty like Ruth's
On whom we can rely.

Sister _____, as each new day unfolds,
We don't know what it contains.
We do know there will be sunshine,
And rainbows that follow the rains.
We know tonight begins a new year for you,
New duties, new hopes, new friends,
And may it be a wonderful year
From beginning to the end.

☆　☆　☆　☆　☆

9. GOOD OF THE ORDER

SISTERHOOD—We can betray it, but we cannot forsake it. We cannot live unto ourselves alone.

A word, a smile, a handshake—or a curse, a scowl, an indifference—each leaves its impression for good or for evil on those with whom we come in contact in our daily lives.

—V. H. L.

☆   ☆   ☆   ☆   ☆

HEAVENLY Father, grant Thy blessing
On our Chapter gathered here;
May Thy truth, our hearts' possession,
Keep our lives from error clear.
May we e'er Thy Light be seeking,
Let no stain our honor mar;
Ever hold in Thy blest keeping,
Our own beloved Eastern Star.

☆   ☆   ☆   ☆   ☆

WHEN we make Love, Truth and Charity
The keynote of our hearts;
And strive in the virtues we teach
To take a living part.
Then will the light of our Order
Send its radiance afar;
And each member will reflect the glory
Of our beautiful Eastern Star.

☆   ☆   ☆   ☆   ☆

SWEETLY your music has swayed us,
Bringing God's love to the soul;

As 'neath our Rainbow's colors soft,
Your notes with melody roll.

☆　　☆　　☆　　☆　　☆

THE purpose of life is to matter, to count, to stand for something, to have it make some difference that we lived at all.　　　　　　　　　　　　　—LEO ROSTEN

☆　　☆　　☆　　☆　　☆

WE come to the shrine of our Eastern Star
As they came to the manger of old;
Some with praise and a prayer in their hearts
And some with gifts of gold.

All came to the manger because they were called
And brought what they could, we are told;
The praise and the prayer were acceptable, too,
And the incense, the myrrh, and the gold.

☆　　☆　　☆　　☆　　☆

MAY we plan and build for the future,
Without hope of personal gain;
Bury all that is selfish within us,
That our Order may achieve and attain.

☆　　☆　　☆　　☆　　☆

IF we all lived up to our great Eastern Star
And proclaimed its teachings near and far;
The world would be different, our lives would be rich,
Whatever our station, wherever our niche.

Live and practice these precepts sublime
Enshrine them in hearts of every clime;

And thus bless the lives of old age and youth
By teaching these virtues—Relief, Love, and Truth.

☆   ☆   ☆   ☆   ☆

MAKE your Chapter splendid,
Be there with a pleasant word,
Let your presence show you love it,
Though your voice may not be heard.

☆   ☆   ☆   ☆   ☆

MAY the Blue ever keep you faithful and true
To convictions of duty and right.

May the Yellow remind you ever to be just
And the White on your path shed its light.

May the Green keep you trustful, with faith to believe,
And the Red give you courage and power.

For with these bright rays of our beautiful Star
Comes strength for each day and each hour.

☆   ☆   ☆   ☆   ☆

AND the Star shall lead us onward
As it did long, long ago;
Where the shepherds sought the Saviour
In the humble stable low.

May the Star we cherish daily
Be transformed in Heaven above;
And each member find his emblem
In the crown of Truth and Love.

☆   ☆   ☆   ☆   ☆

47

Let us never take into the Chapter
Aught of grief or anger or pride,
But always leave at its portals
The strife of the world outside.

Forget the slights of a Sister,
Forgive the wrongs of a Brother;
Remember only the obligation—
To always love one another.

☆　　☆　　☆　　☆　　☆

The prosperity of your Chapter depends on the success and well being of each member.

The happiness of your Chapter depends on the confidence and co-operation you give to your officers.

The reputation your Chapter enjoys in your community depends on the daily example of each member, both in precept and practice.

The strength of your Chapter depends on regular attendance of each member and taking an active part in fulfilling the obligations of the Order.

The privilege of membership includes an important responsibility on the part of members. The officers alone cannot "drive the good vessel along."

☆　　☆　　☆　　☆　　☆

The creed of the Eastern Star is founded upon nobility of character and is associated with human sympathies and understanding. Its treasures are the riches of the human heart and its virtues the foundation of civilization. Its faith is the faith that inspires and illuminates the lives of the humblest, as well as the most exalted of its members. Its charity is as broad as the universe. Let us, therefore, strive earnestly to live up to our Star obligation and thus prove that we are identified with the progress and general welfare of humanity.

☆　☆　☆　☆　☆

"Of all the beautiful pictures
That hang on Memory's wall"—
My visit to your Chapter
Is the very best of all.

☆　☆　☆　☆　☆

O, a wonderful Star is the Eastern Star,
As shining as ever was seen;
With its Adah and Ruth, and its lessons of truth,
And its Esther, superb and serene.

O, a wonderful Star is the Eastern Star
In the glow of its radiant sheen;
With Martha's fair creed, and Electa's rare deeds,
And the faith of the loved Nazarene.

☆　☆　☆　☆　☆

We took the blue of courage
And fashioned a point of the Star;
To this we added humility,
And made a yellow bar.

49

We took the white of loyalty
To kindred, country, friend;
We added faith and unfaltering trust
In God's love, e'en to the end.

For faith we made a green ray,
And for love the flag's red bar;
And so we fashioned the banner—
The beautiful Eastern Star.

☆   ☆   ☆   ☆   ☆

OUR Order stands for peace. We invariably associate the Eastern Star with that Star of Bethlehem which tenderly hovered over the Infant Jesus, whose advent on earth proclaimed the brotherhood of man. Prophets of old foretold His coming as the Prince of Peace. His escort of angels sang the glad refrain, "Peace on Earth, Good Will to Men."

Let us seek to promote the cause of peace and understanding on all occasions—among ourselves as sisters and brothers, as neighbors and fellow citizens, and as fellow human beings of all the earth.

May the day soon come when, by the grace of this Prince of Peace as exemplified in our Order—

> The war drums will throb no longer
> And the battle flags be furled
> In the parliament of men
> The federation of the world.
>
> —*Tennyson.*

☆   ☆   ☆   ☆   ☆

GLORIOUS as is the advancement of our Order, we have but begun to build. With the broadening of our scope comes the opportunity for still greater achievements. We plan, not alone for the present, but we work for the future. As we have profited by the work of the founders, so shall they who follow us profit by our accomplishments and our organization grow increasingly great.

☆　　☆　　☆　　☆　　☆

ON bended knee at the altar we take the sacred obligation of the Order and rise with a new vision of fellowship, imbued with a new sense of our responsibility toward our fellow man, and girded with a stronger faith in God. We, as members of the Order of the Eastern Star, must follow the gleam of the Star in the East and push on to higher and greater things—advocating the universal brotherhood of man, discarding selfishness and petty personal gain, and ever striving to promote and advance the great good of human kind. We must let our light shine that others, seeing our good works, may glorify our Father in Heaven.

☆　　☆　　☆　　☆　　☆

10. FREEMASONRY AND THE EASTERN STAR

(For Master Masons' Night)

HAND in hand our Orders should go
Along life's toilsome road;
Each lending aid to weary ones
Who falter 'neath the load.

Both giving help to pilgrims weak
When traveling near and far;
One by the Compasses led straight,
The other following the Star.

☆   ☆   ☆   ☆   ☆

OURS are Orders that should stand
A light upon our Nation's hill.
A source of inspiration in our land,
A voice forbidding all that's ill.
Its strength—not steel, nor stone, nor wood—
But Justice, Love, and Brotherhood.

☆   ☆   ☆   ☆   ☆

FREEMASONRY and the Eastern Star have many ideals in common. Both work hand in hand in splendid service to humanity, in spreading by precept and example the doctrine of good will to their fellow human beings.

☆   ☆   ☆   ☆   ☆

THAT "in union there is strength" was never demonstrated more clearly than by the splendid achievements of the Eastern Star and Masonic Orders working in unison. In every worthy purpose, the members of the Eastern Star stand ready to help the Masons to the very limit of their strength, and sometimes they accomplish almost the superhuman. They plan just the things that will help the most and never once have they failed to see and respond to the need of help.

☆   ☆   ☆   ☆   ☆

To my mind, the Order of the Eastern Star supplies the crowning glory to Freemasonry. And here I will disclose a Masonic secret. Freemasonry, in its inception, was established upon a threefold foundation—Wisdom, Strength, and Beauty. We have in the Masonic body some wisdom, and considerable strength, but we are rather short on beauty. As I look over this assemblage of beautiful women, I am fully convinced that the Order of the Eastern Star amply supplies that essential element so lacking in Freemasonry—the crowning glory of beauty.

☆   ☆   ☆   ☆   ☆

THE Order of the Eastern Star, by its bounteous ministrations to the needy and distressed, its unostentatious acts of sweet charity, has won its way to recognition as the handmaiden of Freemasonry and is an irresistible power for good, teaching the same principles of Justice, Right and Truth, and educating the heart and intellect.

☆   ☆   ☆   ☆   ☆

LET us give evidence always that we are loyal workers with the Masonic brethren in the service of humanity.

☆　　☆　　☆　　☆　　☆

WE often remind ourselves that the Eastern Star does not claim to be a part of the Masonic Fraternity, yet as the wives, daughters, mothers, widows and sisters of Masons we are tremendously interested in the ideals and aspirations which you cherish. We owe our inception as an Order to a Master Mason and we are dependent upon the growth of your Order for our own growth. We welcome Masons as members of our Order and we rely upon a Mason's aid and counsel in our East.

☆　　☆　　☆　　☆　　☆

11. FRIENDSHIP

WHEN trouble comes your soul to try,
You love the friend who just stands by;
Perhaps there's nothing he can do,
The thing is strictly up to you;
For there are troubles all your own,
And paths your soul must tread alone;
Times when love can't smooth the road,
Nor friendship lift the heavy load.

But just to feel you have a friend,
Who'll stand right by until the end;
Whose sympathy through all endures,
Whose warm handclasp is always yours.
It helps, some way, to pull you through,
Although there's nothing he can do;
And so with fervent heart we cry,
God bless the friend who just stands by.

☆   ☆   ☆   ☆   ☆

TRUE friends, old friends,
Treasuring one's honor;
Kind friends, loving friends,
Were sent by our Heavenly Father.

☆   ☆   ☆   ☆   ☆

IN all our deliberations let us be true to every friendship, loyal to every trust, faithful to every duty, and
steadfast in our faith in each other.

☆   ☆   ☆   ☆   ☆

FRIENDSHIP is a chain of gold,
Shaped in God's all perfect mold;
Each link a smile, a laugh, a tear,
A grip of the hand, a word of cheer.

As steadfast as the ages roll
Binding closer soul to soul;
It matters not how far, how heavy the load,
Sweet is the journey on friendship's road.

☆　☆　☆　☆　☆

OH, the comfort, the inexpressible comfort, of feeling safe with a friend—one with whom we neither have to weigh our thoughts nor measure our words. One to whom we can pour them all out just as they are, chaff and grain together, with the comforting certainty that an understanding heart will take and sift them, keep what is worth treasuring, and then with the breath of kindness blow the chaff away. This is the true essence of friendship.

☆　☆　☆　☆　☆

OUT of the mist comes the fragrance
We breathe in the heart of a rose;
Out of the world come the friendships
That brighten the day at its close;
Out of the heart comes the kindness
To comfort the hour of tears;
Out of time come gently
Our days, our weeks, our years;
Out of the boundless universe

FRIENDSHIP

Comes Divine love without end.
And all of these treasures are blended
In the faithful heart of a friend.

☆　　☆　　☆　　☆　　☆

I DREAMED a wondrous dream one day,
Of a friend so fine and true;
Who'd walk with me mid sunny skies
And skies no longer blue.

A friend who'd fill my life with light
And joy so rich and fine;
Who'd fill me with happiness divine
As I clasped her hand in mine.

Who all my faults would know,
Yet be my friend and stay;
With whom I'd roam and talk and plan
Along life's winding way.

I dreamed this wondrous dream, you see,
With ne'er a thought it might come true;
But God looked down and smiled on me
And I found that friend in you.

☆　　☆　　☆　　☆　　☆

WHEN the evening sky is painted
All crimson by the setting sun;
And birds have ceased to twitter,
Knowing that the day is done.

'Tis then we like to ponder
And forgetting worldly strife,
We realize that love and friendship
Are the greatest things in life.

☆   ☆   ☆   ☆   ☆

TRUE friendship has a sweetness,
That flavors all the years;
It banishes our little cares,
And dries our springing tears;
It sets the heart to singing,
And starts the lips to smile.
Sometimes it seems that friendship
Is what makes this life worth while.

☆   ☆   ☆   ☆   ☆

OUT of the abundance of the heart the mouth speak-
eth. Life can hold no greater treasure than the friends
whose love we share.

☆   ☆   ☆   ☆   ☆

MUCH has been said, written and read,
Of old friends standing true;
That to hold to the old is like hoarding gold,
And old friends are better than new.

To me comes the thought, by experience taught,
Presenting a broader view;
For the same thread of gold we see in the old
Will also be found in the new.

☆   ☆   ☆   ☆   ☆

58

FRIENDSHIP

I'D like to be the sort of friend
That you have been to me;
I'd like to be the help that you've
Been always glad to be.
I'd like to mean as much to you
Each minute of the day;
As you have meant, dear friends of mine,
To me along the way.

☆　　☆　　☆　　☆　　☆

TIME weaves a mystic pattern,
On this queer old loom called life;

His shuttle is the fleeting years,
His warp the joy and strife;

His weel and web, the hopes and dreams,
Good fortune and despair;

But friendship is the golden thread
That makes it all so fair.

☆　　☆　　☆　　☆　　☆

I COULD sail the waters of all the world,
Bitter and wild and blue;
And never find such friends to love
As the friends I have found in you.

I could walk down all the roads of the world
And knock on their doors forever;

But never would find such friends to love.
Never—Never—Never.

☆   ☆   ☆   ☆   ☆

MY heart is an old fashioned garden,
Where the flowers of memory bloom;
Fresh, fragrant and rare,
With dainty, elusive perfume.

But the spot I like best in this garden,
Is the bed of forget-me-nots blue;
Whose wee hearts of gold hold treasures untold
And fond happy memories of you.

☆   ☆   ☆   ☆   ☆

A FRIEND is one who knows you,
Who knows you through and through;
And loves you notwithstanding
What course you may pursue.

Who knows your many virtues,
Your imperfections, too;
Who glories in your triumphs
And helps you to get through.

☆   ☆   ☆   ☆   ☆

GOD bless you, is my wish,
O friends of mine;
May roses bloom along the way,
O friends of mine.

FRIENDSHIP

May your every wish come true,
May joy and plenty come to you,
May victory crown whate'er you do,
O friends of mine.

☆　☆　☆　☆　☆

GOLDEN moments of friendship,
Of loving deeds so true;
Moments painted by mem'ry
In colors of rainbow hue.

Moments that tell of the beauty
All packed in the year that's past;
Beautiful love and friendship
That all through life shall last.

☆　☆　☆　☆　☆

WRITE Life without its friendships,
And who would read it through?
Paint Life without its friendships,
And where is the rainbow hue?
Build Life without its friendships,
And who would live therein?
For Friendship's gleam leads to the goal
That each of us would win.

☆　☆　☆　☆　☆

WHEN evening shades are falling,
At the closing of the day;
And I am just a sitting round
And passing time away.

61

The thought will come to cheer me,
If I'm feeling sort of blue;
A little prayer of gratitude
For crossing paths with you.

☆　☆　☆　☆　☆

YOUR friendship through this year has been
A priceless thing of joy to me;
A golden chain that Time has forged,
Each link a joyous memory.

☆　☆　☆　☆　☆

I CALL my heart the house of friends,
For that is where they dwell;
Where fellowship a hand extends
To all I like so well.

And in this house where sunlight beams
The happy hours through,
There is a room of dreams
Just kept apart for you.

☆　☆　☆　☆　☆

DEAR friends of mine, I often think,
And wonder if you know,
Just what your friendship means to me
Through the days that come and go.

Your handclasp true when skies are dark,
Your faith so deep and strong,

FRIENDSHIP

That make the shadows melt away
And bring blue skies along.

☆   ☆   ☆   ☆   ☆

THE gate of one's friendship garden
Has hinges worn fragile and thin;
But they sing a glad song of welcome
Whenever a friend enters in.

Its latch is bright and shining
From the touch of friends passing through;
And it clicks a note of happiness
Whenever that friend is you.

☆   ☆   ☆   ☆   ☆

THAT friend who serves and seeks for gain
And follows but for form,
Will leave when it begins to rain
And desert you in a storm.

☆   ☆   ☆   ☆   ☆

12. LOVE AND SERVICE

You've taught us Love's sweetest call,
When in our hearts your love began to fall;
E'en in our hearts your song of love will pour,
Deep in our hearts 'twill dwell forever more.

Footsteps may falter, weary grow the way,
Still we'll always hear it day by day;
So till the end, when Life's dim shadows fall,
Love will be found the sweetest song of all.

☆　☆　☆　☆　☆

God bless the rays of sunshine
That smile the clouds away,
And set the Star of fresh-born hope
In someone's sky each day.

God bless the words of kindness
That lift the heart from gloom,
And in Life's barren places
Plant flowers of love to bloom.

☆　☆　☆　☆　☆

Love is no stuff to gather dust on shelves,
The more we give the more we have ourselves.

☆　☆　☆　☆　☆

Truth and love are two of the most powerful things
in the world; and when they both go together they
cannot easily be withstood.

—Ralph Cudworth

☆　☆　☆　☆　☆

64

LOVE AND SERVICE

WOULD that the world were filled with roses,
And every rose were filled with dew;
And every dewdrop filled with love
For each and every one of you—
My Home Folks.

☆   ☆   ☆   ☆   ☆

IN the heart of a rose there's a story sweet,
It's story I'll tell to you;
It's been told o'er and o'er since the world began,
'Tis the sweetest I ever knew.

It tells of a love that's within my heart,
For that's how the story goes;
There is perfumed dew and it's all for you,
In the heart of this red, red rose.

☆   ☆   ☆   ☆   ☆

O, GIVE me Love! Not alone Knowledge and Power!
A Love that can praise the best in the best of us.
A Love that can pity the worst in the worst of us.
A Love that will make us infinitely just and divinely
tender.
A Love that will make Sympathy flower in the Heart
A Love to love all.

☆   ☆   ☆   ☆   ☆

IN the Order of the Eastern Star we have an organization that is founded on the principles of love and service. We follow the precepts of Him whose manger birthplace was lighted by the Star of Bethlehem and whose life of love and service transcends even that brightness.

☆   ☆   ☆   ☆   ☆

65

It is only through service to others,
Giving our truest and best;
That our Star in its glorified splendor
Can lead to a haven of rest.

☆　　☆　　☆　　☆　　☆

Love that is treasured and hidden away,
Brings no increase at end of the day;
But love that is shared spreads far and wide,
And brings contentment at eventide.

☆　　☆　　☆　　☆　　☆

Give love, and love to your heart will flow,
A strength in your hour of need;
Have faith and a score of hearts will show
Their faith in your word and deed.

☆　　☆　　☆　　☆　　☆

True happiness lies only in service
A service that's honest and true;
That gives of its best to each member,
I pray that's been my service to you.

☆　　☆　　☆　　☆　　☆

For 'tis service that merits the best we can give,
Of our faith and our love most sincere;
And we pledge a service that's loyal and true
To our Order we hold so dear.

☆　　☆　　☆　　☆　　☆

For remembrance is the sweetest flower
Of all the earth's perfuming;

LOVE AND SERVICE

Sun and showers, love and friendship
Keep it blooming.

☆   ☆   ☆   ☆   ☆

LET us ever be doing the deeds that are kind,
Eager to help, to heal, and to bind;
Let our feet never tire by night or by day,
Of helping God's weaker ones over Life's way.

In the depths of our eyes let there linger a smile,
Seeing, through love, only good things worth while;
With our hearts ever ready with comfort for others,
Let us live for service, my sisters and brothers.

☆   ☆   ☆   ☆   ☆

WE have gathered here to renew our faith in those
eternal principles upon which our Order is founded.
We are dedicated to a high moral purpose—that of
service.

☆   ☆   ☆   ☆   ☆

No vision and you perish,
No ideal and you're lost;
Your heart must ever cherish
Some faith at any cost.
Some hope, some dream, to cling to,
Some rainbow in the sky;
Some goal for us to work for,
Some service that is high.

☆   ☆   ☆   ☆   ☆

67

13. PATRIOTIC SENTIMENTS

I PLEDGE allegiance to the Flag of the United States of America, and to the Republic for which it stands—one Nation, under God, indivisible, with Liberty and Justice for all.

☆　☆　☆　☆　☆

OH, may these eyes forever rest
Upon the flag I love the best;
Whose diamond stars, bright as the dew,
Adorn a field of azure hue.

The flag with stripes of red and white
Gleam streaks of blood and bars of light;
The flag that whispers home to me
Where'er it waves o'er land or sea.

Recount to me its bravest deeds
And truths higher than all the creeds;
Repeat its message—bold and clear—
"Who trust in God have naught to fear."

Chaste flag of freedom—honor—right—
Wave on thy truth from height to height;
Flag of all flags, I love but thee,
For where thou art is home to me.

☆　☆　☆　☆　☆

WHAT shall I say to you, Old Flag?
You are so grand in every fold,
So linked with the mighty deeds of old,

PATRIOTIC SENTIMENTS

So steeped in blood where heroes fell,
So torn and pierced by shot and shell,
So calm—so still—so firm—so true—
My heart thrills with pride at sight of you,
                                        Old Flag!

☆   ☆   ☆   ☆   ☆

I wish I were gifted as poets are,
With words of silver and gold,
To tell the thoughts that arise in me
For the beautiful flag I hold.

And we, who have seen His Star in the East,
Believe in the wonderful plan
Pledging Bethlehem's Star and America's Flag
For the Brotherhood of Man.

So here's to Old Glory—the grandest Flag
That ever has been unfurled;
Proclaiming us Children of God above
And Sisters to all the world.

☆   ☆   ☆   ☆   ☆

Up to the breeze of the morning I fling you,
Blending your folds with the dawn in the sky.

There let the people behold you and bring you
Love and devotion that never shall die.

Proudly a-gaze at your glory I stand—
Flag o' my land! Flag o' my land!

☆   ☆   ☆   ☆   ☆

Oh, folds of white and scarlet!
Oh, blue field with your silvery stars!
May fond eyes welcome you, willing feet follow you,
Strong arms defend you, warm hearts cherish you,
And the lips of the dying give you their blessing!

☆   ☆   ☆   ☆   ☆

May God bless our Flag. Let it float, and fill
The sky with its beauty. Our heart strings thrill
With the dear, sweet chant of its wind swept bars,
And the swelling chorus of all its clustered stars.

☆   ☆   ☆   ☆   ☆

14. IN MEMORIAM

AND when God calls the dearest ones I love
To dwell with Him in perfect bliss above;
I cannot feel that He has loosed the tie
That bound their human hearts to earth. So I
Find comfort in the thought that they may be
My guardian angels keeping watch o'er me.

At times my heart is sad and I feel the need of cheer,
'Tis then my loved ones seem to hover very near;
I almost feel the touch of each dear hand
Upon my own, to help me understand
I still am theirs and they are mine, e'en though
They dwell in Heaven above and I on earth below.

Not broken ties, but just a veil between
My earthly vision and that world unseen;
A little time to wait, while loved ones there
Keep tender watch, till I may share
Their perfect peace and God's perfect love
That's known to those who dwell with Him above.

☆   ☆   ☆   ☆   ☆

SLEEP on, Beloved, sleep and take thy rest,
Lay down thy weary head upon the Saviour's breast;
We love thee well, but Jesus loves thee best.
Good-night, Beloved, Good-night.

☆   ☆   ☆   ☆   ☆

THE life she lived was true and honest,
Always glad to meet a friend;

Happy hearted and contented,
Faithful to the very end.

Now her earthly strife is over,
No more sorrow, no more care;
Yet our hearts are sad and lonely,
For we miss her everywhere.

☆   ☆   ☆   ☆   ☆

THERE are stars that go out in the darkness
Whose silvery light shineth on;

There are roses whose perfume lingers
When the flowers are faded and gone;

There are hearts full of love and sweetness
Whose life current no longer flows;

Still their goodness lives on with the living
Like the soul of the star and the rose.

☆   ☆   ☆   ☆   ☆

No one hears the doors that open
When they pass beyond our call;
Soft as the dropping petals of a rose,
One by one our loved ones fall.
But the memory of each loved one,
Like the fragrance of the rose,
God sends to linger with us
Till our own life's door shall close.

☆   ☆   ☆   ☆   ☆

IN MEMORIAM

THEY are not gone who pass
Beyond the clasp of hand,
Out from the strong embrace.
They are but come so close
We need not grope with hands,
Nor look to see, nor try
To catch the sound of feet.
They have put off their shoes,
Softly to walk by day
Within our thoughts, to tread
At night our dream-led paths
Of sleep.
They are not lost who find
The sunset gate, the goal
Of all their faithful years.
Not lost are they who reach
The summit of their climb;
The peak above the clouds
And storm.
They are not lost who find
The light of sun and stars—
And God.

☆   ☆   ☆   ☆   ☆

THEY never quite leave us,
Our friends who have passed
Through the gateway eternal
To the sunlight above.

A thousand sweet memories
Are holding them fast

73

To the place they blessed
By their presence and love.

☆　☆　☆　☆　☆

Our Father and our God, we come
In thankfulness and prayer;
For all the blessings of this life
And Thy loving care.

We thank Thee for the friends we have,
Whose love makes life so bright;
And pleadingly we ask that Thou
Wilt guide our steps aright.

Help us to live so near to Thee
That when life's day shall close,
We'll hear at last Thy welcome home,
To rest from all life's woes.

Amen.

☆　☆　☆　☆　☆

One by one, we pass the stations
In the onward march of life;
One by one, through faith we conquer
In the never ending strife.

One by one, we lose the hand clasp
That so warm a welcome gave;
One by one, the voice is silenced
In the stillness of the grave.

IN MEMORIAM

One by one, we miss the faces
Of the friends we once possessed;
One by one, their names are graven
"Ceased to labor"—"Home"—"At rest."

✩　　✩　　✩　　✩　　✩

GOD hath not promised always for you
Flower strewn pathways, bright skies of blue;
God hath not promised sun without rain,
Joy without sorrow, peace without pain.
But He does promise strength from above,
Unfailing sympathy, undying love.

✩　　✩　　✩　　✩　　✩

THERE is only a curtain between us,
Between the beyond and here;
They, whom we call dead, have not left us;
Nay, they were never so near.

Not dead, but promoted,
They have joined the Chapter above;
And blessed by smiles from the Master,
They wait for those whom they love.

✩　　✩　　✩　　✩　　✩

I LIKE to think the clouds are God's curtains—
The blue and white loveliness
With which He drapes His heavenly home—
That human eyes be not blinded
By the beauties within.

Sometimes when the noonday sun
Gives the clouds unearthly radiance,
It seems like angel fingers, pushing back
The swaying curtains of the sky,
That loved ones may look on us once more
Through God's curtains.

☆　☆　☆　☆　☆

WHAT is death? A little parting
In the clouds above us that hide the sun;
A golden vision of souls that love us
And labor done.

☆　☆　☆　☆　☆

WE ask Thee to comfort and bless the sorrowing; draw them to Thee by Thy infinite love. Grant that all our acts and thoughts may be inspired by Thee. May we follow the light of our Star in the East until we, too, lay down the burdens of life, when unto us may be given entrance into the glories of that city not made with hands. Amen.

☆　☆　☆　☆　☆

DRAPING THE ALTAR

By Betty Decker, P.M. (*Arizona*)

As we wait for awhile in this solemn hour,
In the midst of the Labyrinth of our Star
With our Altar draped for the loved ones gone,
This time shall be a personal one.

For as on every Memorial Night
As we pause in our Altar's quiet light,
Each of us sees in his own mind's eye—a face
That holds in our hearts a special place.

Our Eternal Father holds them now,
And our love and His love they share—
May we strive in our lives each passing day
To be worthy of His love and theirs.

☆　☆　☆　☆　☆

15. MISCELLANEOUS

There's a comforting thought at the end of the day,
When I'm weary and lonely and sad;
That sort of takes hold of my hungry heart,
And bids it be merry and glad.

It gets in my soul, and it drives out the blues,
And it thrills me through and through;
It's just a sweet memory, that chants the refrain,
"I'm glad I touched shoulders with you."

I'm glad that I live, that I labor and strive,
For the place that I know I must fill;
I'm thankful for sorrows—I'll meet with a grin
What fortune may bring, good or ill.

I may not have wealth, I may not be great,
But I know I shall always be true;
For I have in my heart the courage you gave
When once I touched shoulders with you.

☆　　☆　　☆　　☆　　☆

Time, like a mighty river, flows on unceasingly. It waits for no one and we must seize our precious opportunities, or they are gone forever.

☆　　☆　　☆　　☆　　☆

Faith, like light, should always be simple and unbending; while love, like warmth, should beam forth on every side, and bend to every necessity of our brethren.
—Martin Luther

☆　　☆　　☆　　☆　　☆

AN old man, traveling a lonely highway,
Came at evening, cold and gray,
To a chasm vast, and deep, and wide;
The sullen stream had no fear for him,
As he crossed in the twilight dim,
But he turned when safe on the other side
And built a bridge to span the tide.

"Old man," said a fellow pilgrim near,
"You are wasting your time by building here,
For you never again will pass this way;
You've crossed the chasm deep and wide,
Why build you this bridge at evening tide?"

The builder lifted his old gray head,
"Good friend, in the path I've come," he said,
"There followed after me today
A youth whose feet must pass this way.
The chasm has been as naught to me,
To that fine youth it may a pitfall be;
He, too, must cross in the twilight dim,
Good friend, I am building that bridge for him."

☆   ☆   ☆   ☆   ☆

WHAT a wonderful time is Life's autumn,
When the leaves of the trees are all gold;
When God fills each day, as He sends it,
With memories priceless and old.

What a treasure house filled with rare jewels,
The friendships of year upon year;

And I pray that this memorable birthday
May bring you most bountiful cheer.

☆   ☆   ☆   ☆   ☆

HOPE

In the darkest hour, there comes a light to those who
sit in the darkness, and a new hope to those, who, in
the quiet hour, will unburden their heavy load and ask
for strength and guidance. It is a wonderful calmness
bringing peace and rest to the weary, and a new
strength to meet the new day unafraid. "Ask, and ye
shall receive"—it is that simple.

—V. H. L.

☆   ☆   ☆   ☆   ☆

We're builders of a better world;
We are workers for a plan,
That seeks to make this good old earth
A happy place for man.

Although we blunder on the way,
And though the road seems long;
We've driven much of care away,
And made more room for song.

We're builders of a better world;
Though brief our time and span,
There shall be more of happiness
Than when our age began.

And though we cannot see it now,
When all is understood,

We shall leave less of wrong behind
And more of what is good.

☆   ☆   ☆   ☆   ☆

THE hills ahead look hard and steep and high,
And often we behold them with a sigh;
But as we near them, level grows the road.
We find on every slope, with every load,
The climb is not so steep nor the top so far;
The hills ahead look harder than they are.

And so with troubles, though they seem so great,
That men complain and fear, and hesitate,
Less difficult is the journey than we dreamed;
It never is so hard as first it seemed.
There never comes a hill, a task, a day,
But as we near them, easier proves the way.

☆   ☆   ☆   ☆   ☆

THE hills of tomorrow are waiting for us,
A little bit farther to go;
And now as we stand on the peaks of today,
A hint of their beauty we know.

We catch but a glimpse of the splendors to be,
The birth of another new day;
And the joys we shall claim and the goals
We shall know, if only we keep on our way.

☆   ☆   ☆   ☆   ☆

LIFE is a privilege, like some rare rose,
The mysteries of the human mind disclose;

What marvels lie in earth and air and sea,
What stories of knowledge await our opening key.

What sunny roads of happiness lead out
Beyond the realm of indolence and doubt;
And what sweet pleasures smile upon and bless
The busy avenues of usefulness.

☆　☆　☆　☆　☆

GENTLENESS

THE world wastes with evil things. Let us open our
hearts; open them to hope, open them wide to let in
gentleness which can change a harsh and bitter world—
a world that is desolate for faith and hope and joy.
Comely gentleness can bring a song of joy that fairly
rings in the presence of God.

—V. H. L.

☆　☆　☆　☆　☆

FRATERNITY is a lovely plant
That grows in a garden place;
A plant that can fill your life with peace,
With fragrance and charm and grace.
A plant that can lend its color rare
To brighten the darkest sky;
A plant that can banish loneliness
And send away despair.

But whether it blooms depends on you,
For the plant is a fragile one;
You must warm its leaves with the golden light

Of affection's shining sun;
You must plant its roots in the fertile soil
Of a thousand thoughtful deeds;
And must keep it free of distrust and doubt,
For distrust and doubt are weeds.

☆　☆　☆　☆　☆

Just a bit of happiness,
Just a bit of mirth,
That is what we need
On this queer old earth;
Wealth has wings and flies away,
Fairest things grow old;
But a little bit of happiness,
That is just pure gold.

☆　☆　☆　☆　☆

We have met, and kindness round us
Hath a wreath of beauty twined;
Peace and all good-will hath bound us,
Heart and heart, and mind to mind.

☆　☆　☆　☆　☆

I know a place where the sun is like gold,
And the flower blooms burst with snow;
And down underneath is the loveliest nook,
Where the four-leaved clovers grow.

One leaf is for Faith, and one is for Hope,
And one is for Love, you know;

And God put another one in for Luck,
If you search you may find where they grow.

But you must have Faith, and you must have Hope,
And you must love and be strong; and so
If you work, if you wait, you can find the place
Where the four-leaved clovers grow.

☆   ☆   ☆   ☆   ☆

IF all that we say in a single day,
With never a word left out,
Were printed each night, in clear black and white,
'Twould prove queer reading, no doubt.

And then just suppose, e'er our eyes we should close,
We must read the whole record through;
Then wouldn't we sigh, and wouldn't we try
A great deal less talking to do?

And I more than half think, that many a kink,
Would be smoother in Life's tangled thread,
If half that we say in a single day
Were left forever unsaid.

☆   ☆   ☆   ☆   ☆

THE law of things is that they who tamper with veracity, from whatever motive, are tampering with the vital force of human progress.

—JOHN MORLEY.

☆   ☆   ☆   ☆   ☆

IF you are tempted to repeat
A tale someone to you has told
About another, make it pass,
Before you speak, "three gates of gold."

These narrow gates: first, "is it true?"
Then, "is it needful?" In your own mind
Give a truthful answer. The next
Is the last and closest, "is it kind?"

And if, to reach your lips at last,
It passes through these gateways three,
Then you may tell the tale, nor fear
What the result of speech may be.

☆   ☆   ☆   ☆   ☆

IT is not the man who growls all day
And says that the world's unfair;
Who thinks the trials that come his way
Are doubly more than his share;
Who drops his pack with a heavy heart
As soon as real trouble begins;
And cries with a frown, "You've got me down!"
He is not the man who wins.

The man who wins is the man who will dare
To laugh in misfortune's face;
Who pushes ahead with a right good air,
Determined to conquer the place;
With a thankful heart for the smiling sky,
And a thankful heart for the rain;

85

He finds each day will more than pay
For yesterday's toil and pain.

☆   ☆   ☆   ☆   ☆

ONE does not leave a convivial party before closing time.
—WINSTON CHURCHILL.

☆   ☆   ☆   ☆   ☆

THE Master's painting is made day by day;
He is painting the worn out world away.
With a master hand and a magic brush,
He is painting the hour of twilight hush.

Changing the landscape of old Mother Earth,
With a bright new garb and a strange new birth.
He is painting his glory on hillside and glen,
Painting good will in the hearts of men.

☆   ☆   ☆   ☆   ☆

'TIS the burdens you help another to bear
That make your own seem light;
'Tis the danger seen for another's feet
That shows you the path to right;
'Tis the good you do each passing day,
With a heart sincere and true;
For, giving the world your very best,
Its best will come back to you.

☆   ☆   ☆   ☆   ☆

IF I could write one little word
Upon the hearts of men,

I'd dip into the font of Love
And write with golden pen:
>   *Fraternity.*

The angel throng would sing a song,
The sweetest ever heard;
If they could read in human hearts
That precious little word:
>   *Fraternity.*

☆   ☆   ☆   ☆   ☆

PARTY-GIVING is loving. It is giving. It is sharing. It is everybody's chance to light a little candle in the sometimes gloomy corners of the world.
>   —ELSA MAXWELL.

☆   ☆   ☆   ☆   ☆

BUILD thee more stately mansions, O my soul,
As the swift seasons roll!
Leave thy low-vaulted past!
Let each new temple, nobler than the last,
Shut thee from Heaven with a dome more vast,
Till thou at length art free,
Leaving thine outgrown shell by life's unresting sea!
>   —OLIVER WENDELL HOLMES.

☆   ☆   ☆   ☆   ☆

NOT what we have, but what we use;
Not what we see, but what we choose.
These are the things that mar or bless
The sum of human happiness.

87

Not as we take, but as we give;
Not as we pray, but as we live.
These are the things that make for peace
Both now and after Time shall cease.

☆ ☆ ☆ ☆ ☆

DEAR LORD, in the battle that lasts through life,
I ask but a field that is fair;
A chance that is equal with all in the strife,
A courage to do and to dare.

And if I should win, let it be by the code,
With my faith and my honor held high;
And if I should lose, let me stand by the road
And cheer as the winners go by.

☆ ☆ ☆ ☆ ☆

THERE'S a Road Beyond Tomorrow
Where the skies are blue again;
There is hope to follow sorrow
Just as sunshine follows rain.
And although the rain is falling
And the skies are gray, not blue,
On the Road Beyond Tomorrow
God is waiting there for you.

☆ ☆ ☆ ☆ ☆

MARCH swiftly on. Yet err not from the way
Where all the wise of old have trod,
The path of faith made by the sons of God.
Follow the marks they have set beside

The narrow, cloud-swept track. Be it thy guide.
Follow and honor what the past has gained,
And forward still, that more may be attained.

☆　☆　☆　☆　☆

WE will ever strive to strengthen the ties of affection,
promote the prosperity of our Order, and protect its
unity, integrity and strength by maintaining the truest
fraternal spirit.

☆　☆　☆　☆　☆

A LITTLE praise for what we've done
Delights the heart, uplifts the soul;
Inspires us for the tasks begun
And leads us to the goal.

☆　☆　☆　☆　☆

FOR shelter is done when the night is o'er,
And bread lasts only a day;
But the sound of the voice and the clasp of the hand
Will live in the soul alway.

☆　☆　☆　☆　☆

MAY His Star in the East illumine the way
Along your path with pure and shining light;
May every step in life's journey bright
Help you to stand for Truth and Right.

☆　☆　☆　☆　☆

OMISSION

I COULD have taken time today
To give a word of praise.

But, no, I was too busy
(Or, so I thought)
To listen to another's woes.
I gained but little in my foolish haste
And could have given much
By just a word of praise.

—V. H. L.

☆　☆　☆　☆　☆

LIFE is a story in volumes three:
The Past, the Present, the Yet-to-Be.
The first we've written and laid away,
The second we're reading day by day,
The third, the last of volume three,
Is locked from sight. God keepeth the key.

☆　☆　☆　☆　☆

COURTESY, that magic thing,
Is swifter than a bird on wing;
It wields its wand, and lo! we see
All things are as they ought to be.

It sheds its ray of love and light,
And banishes from earthly sight
All petty things, and then behold!
Its value is, indeed, untold.

☆　☆　☆　☆　☆

THERE is no conquest all complete,
No stopping place for human feet,
No final goal.

Onward and upward do we ascend
And none of us shall see the end
Of glory's scroll.
But small and trivial is the past,
It is the future that is vast!

☆　☆　☆　☆　☆

WE may not carry with us into the life beyond aught of earth's gold or jewels, but we may enter it with rich gifts for our King if we bear the gold of a well-lived earthly life and the fair jewels of loving service to our fellow man.

☆　☆　☆　☆　☆

SILENTLY, one by one, in the infinite meadows of heaven Blossom the lovely stars, the forget-me-nots of the angels.

—LONGFELLOW.

☆　☆　☆　☆　☆

THE real essence of the fraternal spirit is to be ever mindful of the welfare of others, to bring cheer and gladness into other lives. So let us put heart and soul into every handclasp, greet each other as sisters and brothers, and enjoy life's sunshine together.

☆　☆　☆　☆　☆

WE dream of universal brotherhood. We are longing and striving for it. With the eye of faith we eagerly peer into the future. Dimly we see the golden fringe of the mantle of glory which will some day enfold the masses of humanity as they stand united.

☆　　☆　　☆　　☆　　☆

ANOTHER beautiful month of June is with us. Clad in living green is the whole countryside. Spread over the earth in beauty and fragrance are blossoms of countless varieties, the radiant evidence of the benevolence of our God. Flowers are truly "Stars of the Earth," the "Forget-me-nots of the Angels" and the "Delight of Mankind." We see them everywhere, lifting their heads in pride at accomplishing their chief purpose of making us happy.

☆　　☆　　☆　　☆　　☆

SOMEONE has said, "coming together is beginning, working together is progress, keeping together is success." We have come together, we have worked together, now let us keep together and succeed. Yesterday is gone, tomorrow may never come, but today is here, so let us use it. Let us turn our faces toward a new day of deeper understanding. Let us, as men and women who have learned the great truths of our Order, advance only things of lasting value. Let us live up to our responsibilities as members of the Eastern Star.

☆　　☆　　☆　　☆　　☆

WHEN all the other months had dressed in blue and
　　　gold and green,
Each one of them more beautiful than any reigning
　　　queen;

October stood a bit apart and flung her white arms wide,
And, "I will be a gypsy month—a gypsy month," she
    cried.

"My hair will be the mist that curls about the purple
    hills,
And I will sound a vagrant call—a call that lures and
    thrills;
And I will wear a scarlet gown, with flowing russet
    sleeves,
And I will dance a gypsy dance among the whirling
    leaves."

And so it is. Though other months may sing a sweeter
    lay,
Though joy and happiness may meet as dream day
    touches day;
October flings her white arms wide and stands a bit
    apart
With wonder in her lifted eyes, and romance in her
    heart.

☆   ☆   ☆   ☆   ☆

For any gift God gives to me I cannot fully pay;
Gifts are most mine which I most give away.
His gifts are like the flowers which show their right to
    stay
By giving all their bloom and fragrance away.
Riches are not in land or gold, estates or marts;
The only wealth worth having is found in human hearts.

☆   ☆   ☆   ☆   ☆

A SEAL be placed upon our lips—for words, once spoken, are beyond recall. Only He alone, who sees all things, can know the infinite pain and evil that follow in the wake of unkind words and acts. Therefore, let each of us put into practice constantly the principles we profess, lest the things that we say, however noble and fine they may sound, are as "tinkling cymbals and sounding brass."

☆   ☆   ☆   ☆   ☆

A LAUGH is just like sunshine,
It freshens all the day;
It tips the peak of life with light,
And drives the clouds away.
The soul grows glad that hears it,
And feels its courage strong;
A laugh is just like sunshine
For cheering folks along.

☆   ☆   ☆   ☆   ☆

LET us go about our work in the consciousness that the all wise Father is the head of our great Fraternity, the unseen guest at all our meetings, the unseen listener in all our deliberations—and He will reward us accordingly.

☆   ☆   ☆   ☆   ☆

WE come in a spirit of earnest purpose to review our yesterdays and to plan for our tomorrows. Let us strive constantly in the hope that the shuttle of time may weave the glowing threads of blue, yellow, white, green and red into a splendid fabric of charity, truth, and loving kindness. Let each of us go forth determined anew to be constant in endeavor and faithful to duty.

☆ ☆ ☆ ☆ ☆

SPRINGTIME—so appropriately symbolic of the glorious present and our hope for the future. The time when mankind turns away from the darkness, doubts and uncertainties, the perplexities and disappointments, as represented by Winter. When we take on new hope, revive inspiration, renew the faith, and outline more clearly the high ideals of life. It is then we take fresh courage and face the future with confidence.

☆ ☆ ☆ ☆ ☆

A PRAYER FOR THE HOME

God bless this house and all within it,
Let no harsh spirit enter in it;
Let none approach who would betray,
None with bitter word to say.
Shield it from harm and sorrow's sting,
Let here the children's laughter ring;
Grant that these friends from year to year,
Shall build their happiest memories here.

God bless this house and those who love it,
Fair be the skies which bend above it;
May never anger's thoughtless word
Within these sheltering walls be heard.
May all who rest beside this fire
And then depart, glad thoughts inspire;

And make those feel who close the door,
Friendship has graced their home once more.

God bless this house and those who keep it,
In the sweet oils of gladness steep it;
Endow these walls with lasting wealth,
The light of love, the glow of health;
The palm of peace, the charm of mirth,
Good friends to sit around the hearth;
And with each nightfall perfect rest—
Here let them live their happiest.

☆　　☆　　☆　　☆　　☆

A FEW words, well and truly said,
Will greater good impart,
Than hosts of words that reach the head,
But never touch the heart.

☆　　☆　　☆　　☆　　☆

A SALUTE TO SIDE-LINERS
—FAY MAY, P.M. (*Ohio*)

(*This may be read by the W.M. or divided into parts for officers*)

A Chapter must have officers, our ritual to portray,
We must have someone to lead the way.

We need our past officers, their experience to share,
But the light of our Star doesn't stop there.

In fact, our Star would not shine very bright
If there were no side-liners to need its light.

Side-liners give us our reason to be—
They are the heart of the Chapter, we agree.

The members on the side line greet us with a smile,
Their interest and acceptance make everything worth-
     while.

When we need them, side-liners give a helping hand,
With their pleasure in mind, all our meetings are
     planned.

Side-liners give their faith and love, and are loyal to
     those who serve,
This priceless gift we cherish and hope to deserve.

With fidelity to each other, in our theme we all share,
And set this evening aside to tell our side-liners that
     we care.

☆   ☆   ☆   ☆   ☆

PARTING SONG

By CORNELIA SCHATMEYER, P.M. (*New Jersey*)

Tune: "Just a Song at Twilight"

JUST a prayer in closing,
Welling from the heart,
Wishing you safe journey,

Which you now will start.
Wend your way with safety
On the ride back home,
May you know God's blessing
Wher'er you roam,
Wherever you ma-ay roam.

Through the dark and shadows,
God will send his light
To loved ones and sisters
Here with us tonight.
And His love will bless them
On life's journey, too,
As we love each other,
He'll love us true,
He will love us true.

☆   ☆   ☆   ☆   ☆

A THANK YOU VERSE

By CORNELIA SCHATMEYER, P.M. (*New Jersey*)

I'VE enjoyed my visit here tonight
In _____ Chapter's meeting room
Where friendly faces line the walls,
Where smile and handclasp banish gloom.

It's here that sisters seek to learn
The lessons of our Order fine;
It's here that we share moments sweet,
Where love and happiness combine.

With melody, the evening sped,
In memory it will remain,

And with a hope that's most sincere,
I hope that I may come again.

So as we close another page
Upon the fleeting hours that pass,
I'll leave this wish for each of you:
May happiness be yours—to last.

We never like to say good-bye,
But parting moments can be sweet
If we will but remember that
Within these walls again we'll meet.

God bless you each and every one,
And remember that until the end,
Our worries and our cares are light
When we share the burdens of a friend.

☆   ☆   ☆   ☆   ☆

QUESTIONS, QUESTIONS

OH, the wonder of a child's mind,
How quickly do they learn.
"What's that?" and "Why?" time after time
They grope for knowledge in the grown-up world.
And, do we take time to give answer
To these ceaseless questions?
Or have we forgotten that once, we, too,
    could not understand
The inconsistencies of grown-ups' lessons?

—V. H. L.

☆   ☆   ☆   ☆   ☆

THANKSGIVING

Count our blessings while we may
Is such sound advice;
Thank the Lord the livelong day
From the moment we arise.

Give thanks for good health, to be exact,
And a roof over our head,
For a family intact,
And sufficient daily bread.

—R.W. Luba G. Resnick

☆   ☆   ☆   ☆   ☆

BIRTHDAYS

Birthdays are happy days
No matter what the weather—
The gifts from all, and candles, tall,
When families get together.

—Etta May Gibbany

☆   ☆   ☆   ☆   ☆

THE INVISIBLE CHURCH

By Cornelia Schatmeyer, P.M. (*New Jersey*)

There's a steeple built of praying hands
That are raised to God on high,
Many praying hands that reach
In supplication to the sky.

There are stained glass windows, softly lit
Of eyes that know the Truth,
Eyes that worship, eyes that love,
Eyes of age and youth.

The foundations are laid on bended knee
And obedience to the Word,
On the head bowed low and the listening ear
When lessons old are heard.

Through the pulsing of the human heart,
And in kindness to each other
The music of the church rings out
As we love one another.

There are no pews, no roof above,
No walls to join the whole,
Yet, many meet their Master here
On the altar of the soul.

☆　☆　☆　☆　☆

SPECIAL RECOGNITION FOR RAINBOW GIRLS

By Dorothy Trimble, P.M. (*Indiana*)

When someone is selected
To wear a crown,
It can mean much more
Than fame and renown.

When honors come
Along the way,

The memories of them
Will always stay.

Being chosen means someone
Has trusted you
To perform the tasks
You were elected to do.

For the Rainbow Order
Leads the way
In choosing what's best
For every day.

All of the colors
Of the Rainbow's hue
Are symbols of something
We find in you.

You are the treasure we found
At our rainbow's end
Our Rainbow Queen—
And our trusted friend.

☆　　☆　　☆　　☆　　☆

CHRISTMAS EVE

By Margaret Melissinos (*New York*)

The velvet night was clear and still;
　　The air was clean and good;
The while, upon a distant hill
　　Three shrouded shepherds stood.

They stood in wonderment, and awe,
  As carved against the sky,
And marveled at the star they saw
  Whose brightness dimmed the eye.

One hushed voice spake, "What can it be
  Whose light outshines the moon?
The brilliance of the star we see
  Makes shadows of the noon!"

And suddenly there did appear
  An angel from above,
Whose gentle words cast out their fear,
  "This is a sign of love.

"I bid you follow where it leads,
  For there glad tidings wait,
For God did grant His only Son
  In birth upon this date."

A heavenly host was heard to sing,
  "Good will toward all men,
And peace on earth." They all took wing.
  The sight did vanish then.

The shepherds whispered, "Let us now go
  Even unto Bethlehem,
And find this Babe that God did know
  Whose love glows as a gem."

And following the light above,
  They did proceed in haste,

103

Until they found this Child of Love,
  The manger that he graced.

And, yea, the darkness of the tomb
  Had ruled upon the earth,
'Til lovely Mary's blessed womb
  Had giv'n the Savior birth.

But now all brightness did prevail
  And music filled the air:
The glorious end of long travail
  Was echoed everywhere.

And gifts of incense and of myrrh
  Were brought from miles around;
Great visitors from far and near
  All trod the sacred ground.

The beasts stood by; the donkey, cow,
  The camel and the ass;
Their beastly wit knew not of how
  This thing had come to pass.

Nor any man did know much more
  Than that his God was good;
And that His son would show the door
  To Love and Brotherhood.

That Christmas Eve meant love and joy
  For all the world to know;
The birth of one small baby boy
  Had made the heavens glow.

As God did show the Three Wise Men
   Their beacon from afar,
All one need do, is look up, then,
   To find the Eastern Star.

☆   ☆   ☆   ☆   ☆

POEMS

   By ELEANOR B. WESSNER, P.M. (*Minnesota*)

CAN I BE A STAR?

I FEEL so helpless when I think
How the Light of the World could not make people
   drink,
From the cup of love
Sent from God above.

Now I humbly sit at the point of a Star
Wondering about my light, and how far
It can shine in this world of strife,
And if I am worthy of this honor in life.

If I were Adah, would my heart be true
To my father's vow and what he must do?
How can I answer? I do not know,
But I fervently hope I have courage to show.

Could I be Ruth, devoted, serene,
Willing to toil, willing to glean

To lighten for others their burdens and grief?
I hope this could be my devotion, my belief.

As Queen Esther, would I forget
Who were my people, and selfishly let
Their cries go unheard?
Or would I risk all by a word?

Will I always be faithful and true,
As Martha could steadfastly do?
Or will I want my will to be done,
Instead of that of the Father and Son?

To be Electa, I must forget myself,
And take a cup down from my shelf,
Fill, and refill with whatever others need,
Give graciously, and wish them Godspeed.

These are the tasks confronting me now.
Let me be able to fulfill my vow
To do for others each precious day,
That they may be happy I came their way.

☆　　☆　　☆　　☆　　☆

THE ALTAR

An altar represents the place
Where one meets God face to face.
For one cannot approach and stand
Without feeling Him take your hand.

The heart beat roars within the breast,
And one wonders, can we meet the test
Of life as He will decree,
For each of us, you and me?

How few of us kneel
To confess what we feel,
To repeat weaknesses and fears
And cleanse our soul with salty tears?

He waits upon us, hoping
We will seek and not go groping,
But implore Him at His altar
For strength lest we falter.

☆　☆　☆　☆　☆

OBLIGATION

AN obligation is a solemn duty,
Filling the heart with devotion and beauty.
And those who seek truth through love
Receive guidance from above.

But, as a flame left untended,
Moral fires soon are ended.
The light grows faint, the purpose weak,
And in testimony we seldom speak.

Thus, the need to re-inspire,
Receiving strength from the Eternal Fire

107

Which rose in the East for all to see,
Promising light 'til eternity.

☆ ☆ ☆ ☆ ☆

IF ONE SHOULD FALL

IF one should fall,
It is the fault of all.
For we, as sisters, should know
Of others' needs that may not show.

No one should feel alone with no ties.
But they may not realize
How strong is their need to confide.
They run from life and hide.

The Eastern Star gives a steady light
Showing the path that is right.
Some take the light and become strong,
Others need a loving friend to go along.

Try then to be the friend,
Who starts with love to try to mend
The hurts life deals to another.
God expects this of a sister and a brother.

☆ ☆ ☆ ☆ ☆

ADAH
A lonely figure stands by an altar
To faithfully fulfill a vow.

But fearful lest he falter
He prays, "Lord sustain me now."

A loving daughter bids farewell with a kiss,
She knows her duty well.
Devotion deep and true as this
Demands discipline few can tell.

We strive to find strength for each trial,
And devotion for one's duty.
The cup we raise, though a bitter vial,
Leads to everlasting beauty.

☆   ☆   ☆   ☆   ☆

RUTH

HER heart was troubled
And filled with grief.
But her faith was doubled
As she passed each sheaf.

She was humble and kind,
She sought no glory for her task.
And there came a peace of mind
Ever greater than she had asked.

Know ye, therefore, if ye walk in truth,
Willing to serve another,
In you will shine the radiance of Ruth
Seen by each sister and brother.

☆   ☆   ☆   ☆   ☆

ESTHER

In regal splendor she came
To ask favor of the King.
She played a dangerous game,
Her life, an expendable thing.

Her people were to die
Unless she took courage and spoke.
She knew she must try,
God had placed on her this yoke.

"What wilt thou, my wife?
Your wish, my command."
"Give my people new life,
Then will I honor any demand."

Life is demanding, sometimes cruel
As we trace its course.
But follow the Golden Rule
With its promise of Divine force.

☆   ☆   ☆   ☆   ☆

MARTHA

While Martha wept,
Her brother died.
Yet, faith she kept
Though sorely tried.

Then Jesus came
To soothe her pain.

110

MISCELLANEOUS

He'd healed the lame
And Lazarus would live again.

"Believest thou this?"
Life is an eternal flame,
Rekindled after death's kiss
To live in Jesus' name.

Would that we all
Saw death as a beginning.
And answer the call
To new life free of sinning.

☆　☆　☆　☆　☆

ELECTA
ELECTA took
The cross to her breast
And with never a backward look
Became a symbol to the rest.

The church is Electa by name,
Her emblem, the cross.
She sustained all who came
To mourn the Saviour's loss.

"Love one another," her plea.
And if ye believe,
He shall set ye free
From all things that ye grieve.

☆　☆　☆　☆　☆

BE THEN ASHAMED

SISTERS are we in name,
In the heart it is not always the same.
To all, we speak and smile
But are we holding a grudge all the while?

We are not happy for others,
Oft we covet honor given our brothers.
We never seem to learn
Respect is something we must earn.

Do we love to be clever, rather than kind,
Use cutting remarks to show off our mind?
Do we daily trod our thoughtless way
Hurting others with what we say?

Often our foolish pride
Breeds pettiness we ought to hide.
With sly remark of hidden meaning,
We sow hurts for later gleaning.

Be then ashamed, sister or brother,
If ye have not love, one for another.
For ye have taken a sacred vow—
It is not too late to remember it now.

☆   ☆   ☆   ☆   ☆

16. THE YEAR IN ADDRESSES

1. Thanks to Installing Officers.
2. Incoming Matron's Address.
3. Incoming Patron's Address.
4. Welcome to Distinguished Guest.
5. Welcome to the District Deputy Grand Matron.
6. Our Chapter Birthday.
7. Address on Obligation Night.
8. Our Unspoken Obligations.
9. Worthy Matron's Address to Master Masons.
10. Past Matrons' and Past Patrons' Night.
11. Response to Welcome.
12. Farewell Tribute to Worthy Matron.
13. Matron's Farewell Address.
14. Patron's Farewell Address.

1. WORTHY MATRON'S THANKS TO INSTALLING OFFICERS ON INSTALLATION NIGHT

With Presentation of Gifts
By R. W. SYLVIA SYD ENGEL (*New York*)

You have all played a very important part in our Installation ceremonies, and have helped to make this evening an enjoyable one for our guests. For me, you have done much more. You have each given me, as the new presiding Matron of ＿＿＿＿＿＿ Chapter, a part of yourselves that I shall never forget.

You, ＿＿＿ (*name of Chaplain*), have given me a prayer to carry in my heart, to give me the courage to go on when skies look gray.

You, ＿＿＿ (*Marshal and Ass't Marshal*), have shown me the right road on which to travel; a path of kindness and sincerity—of justice and understanding.

And, ＿＿＿＿＿＿ (*Installing Officer*), last, but not least, you have always been a sincere friend of this Chapter and all its members. The spirit of the Order of the Eastern Star—a spirit of good will, sincerity, and friendship, is imbedded in your soul, and is visible in your every action. This spirit you have transmitted to my heart through your confidence in me and, now, more than ever, do I value your friendship.

To each of you, may I present this slight token of my gratitude and hope that through the year of 19＿＿, I may look to you for guidance and friendship. With all my heart, I thank you.

☆　☆　☆　☆　☆

2. INCOMING MATRON'S ADDRESS

My heart is filled to overflowing with gratitude that my sisters and brothers have advanced me, step by step, until tonight you have conferred upon me the honor of the East in our Chapter.

Fully realizing my limitations, I bring to you a firm faith in God, devotion to our Order, and zeal and determination to do my life's best in carrying on the work in the spirit of our founders and my predecessors.

Life is made up, not always of great sacrifices or tasks, but of the little things in which smiles and kindly thought, with small obligations fulfilled habitually, make up the important whole.

If the wheel of life is constructed with the hub and center of service and made to revolve on the axle of love, it may be traced to the uttermost parts of the earth, however dim may be the imprint. So it is with the little courtesies of daily life.

Our slogan for the year may well be: Love and Service. Neither is complete alone. Together, they make up a perfect and beautiful whole. When we have real love, the right sort of love, we are eager to serve and carry out the Master's command: Take sweet counsel together and walk in the house of God in company.

With fraternal love as my guiding thought, my heart is filled with appreciation of the honor you have conferred upon me, and to one and all I extend sincere thanks. You have my earnest pledge to give my best efforts to the welfare of our Chapter and our Order and I shall consecrate my time and my strength to its service.

☆   ☆   ☆   ☆   ☆

3. INCOMING PATRON'S ADDRESS

GREETINGS:

In the usual course of human events, there are occasions in our life's journey—from the time of our entrance into the world until that time when we are called to wrap the draperies of our couch about us and lie down in eternal sleep—which influence our existence and enrich our experience.

In my own life, the occasion which stands out predominantly and represents the highest honor ever bestowed, is the trust and confidence expressed in your selection of myself as your Worthy Patron. It means to me the delightful realization of a worthy ambition.

In assuming the duties of my new office, I am deeply sensible of its time honored traditions, as well as its glorious opportunities for helpful service. I am also conscious of the corresponding obligations which are attendant upon this honorable position and I shall constantly strive to do all that I can for our Order whose tenets and principles are so impressed upon my heart.

Due to human frailty, mistakes are apt to occur and I shall appreciate your viewing in fraternal spirit any act of mine concerning which you may hold a different opinion. It is my sincere desire to work in harmonious accord and I wish to thank all of the sisters and brothers for giving me this opportunity.

☆　☆　☆　☆　☆

4. WELCOME TO DISTINGUISHED GUEST

OUR heads and our hearts are in unison today in greeting and extending a warm welcome to you, our guest.

We welcome you heartily and lovingly—not only because you are with us in an official capacity, but also because your own personality has dignified your work in the Order and we love you.

The fact that you occupy such a distinguished position of honor and trust signifies that you have the true spirit of enthusiasm for the work of the Order and have manifested outwardly those inner virtues recommended to us by St. Paul: long-suffering, forbearance, charity, truth, hope, and love.

We realize that your high station carries with it deep understanding of the struggles and aspirations of the Order and your presence here lends us courage and strength, provides us with the stimulus to strive with renewed effort to achieve greater good in the future.

The joy of your visit does not cease with the close of this meeting but will continue to enrich our lives and our Chapter.

☆　☆　☆　☆　☆

5. WELCOME TO DISTRICT DEPUTY GRAND MATRON

DEAR Worthy District Deputy Grand Matron, I bid you a most joyous welcome. The word "welcome" is the keynote of hospitality, of open doors, of friendly greetings, and of warm handclasps. All of these we extend to you and hope your visit with us will be pleasant and memorable to you, as it will be to us.

Throughout the year we have followed your visits in the District with loving hearts and earnest hopes, always eager to hear news of your successful visits. And now that it is the night of your official visit to us, we offer you our homage and our love.

We esteem it an honor and a joy and a privilege to welcome you to our midst, to have you meet with us in our family temple, and to gather about our ancient Altar, fragrant with the incense of many loving hearts.

☆　　☆　　☆　　☆　　☆

6. OUR CHAPTER BIRTHDAY

By R.W. SYLVIA SYD ENGEL (*New York*)

In the name of _____ Chapter No. ____, Order of the Eastern Star, I take great pleasure in welcoming you to our __th birthday party.

It is customary, upon the celebration of the birthday of our Chapter, to review in various 'modi operandi' the life of (*name of Chapter*) from the day of its formation up to the present.

As I stand here this evening, I am impressed with the thought that ours is a rather unusual family. Our home has always been furnished in the same manner, representing the formation of our emblematic star. Through the years some of our sisters and brothers have strayed from the fold, but our family has steadily increased despite this fact. But the singularity to which I refer, which exists in THIS family, is that the name has always remained the same, _____ Chapter, although the heads of the family have changed each year. Some of you might think that this constant change may have caused the children (us) to become unstable, undisciplined, unrestrained or, perhaps irresolute of purpose. This, my good friends, would be an erroneous conclusion.

Quite to the contrary, this variation of parents, so to speak, has enabled the children (members) to glean from their assorted parentage a great deal more in the way of intelligence, fine characteristics, diversified learning,

119

and sincerity of purpose than could ever possibly be acquired from just one set of parents.

We boast of such highly gifted orators among our parents as (*insert appropriate names*) Past Matrons and Past Patrons, all of whose eloquence has been reflected in several of the junior members of the family. Others, such as _____ have imbued us with the same characteristics as they manifested—a sincerity of purpose which has made us strive to live up to their standards. We delight in the memory of hours spent with _____ whose spontaneous facility of expression has instilled in the Chapter family the desire to attain at least a semblance of his ability. We bow to the happy memories instilled in our hearts by _____ and _____, as fine a set of parents as our Chapter has ever known.

And this, my dear sisters and brothers, brings us to the present at which time you are quite well aware of the splendor of our present family. The cloak of parenthood lies gracefully upon their shoulders, and they are contributing the dignity, strength, inspiration, and sincerity necessary to the life of our Chapter family.

These are the builders of _____ Chapter. May we all be spared to continue our fraternal family with at least as much happiness and success as we have known in the past, and to keep the name of _____ Chapter aglow in the Eastern Star sky.

☆　☆　☆　☆　☆

7. ADDRESS ON OBLIGATION NIGHT

By Mrs. J. W. Holley (*No. 986–Texas*)

Tonight we are centering our thoughts on our Eastern Star Obligation.

Let us think for a moment what this word *obligation* means. It is defined as: "An act of binding ones self to DO or NOT do something; a promise."

When we were iniatiated into the Order of the Eastern Star we made a promise that we would do, and would not do, some specific things. The easiest part of the Obligation was taking it.

Most of us in this room have repeated the marriage vows, or promises. The more we love our partner in marriage the easier it becomes for us to keep those vows. The more we love our Eastern Star the easier it is for us to keep our obligation. It is one way we may, as individuals, express our love.

Every obligation should be a solemn one. Every obligation should be sincere. Each one of us had to meet certain qualifications before we could become members of the Order of the Eastern Star. Each one of us paid the same amount of money to become members of this Chapter. As individuals we each entered through the same channels, even through the same door, being reminded by the Conductress that we came of our own free will. Then followed the actual taking of this beautiful, helpful Obligation, as we were being initiated into this Order.

121

We remember, as we repeated these words for the first time, led by a Worthy Patron, that we were in a kneeling position, facing our Altar, on which rested an open Bible, and each of us held a small Bible in our own hands.

No one can take this OBLIGATION for another.

Each candidate makes his own individual promise.

Each member must keep his own OBLIGATION.

When we take an obligation, we make a promise.

What were some of the promises we made?

These are the things we guard as our secrets.

We pledge loyalty, and we promise to give. We promise to be helpful and to be discreet. Do we remember the spirit of giving, and that of loyalty? Do we keep a discreet silence at all times?

Each part of our beautiful OBLIGATION can be beneficial to us, and to others. We promise nothing that can hurt us, but a lot that can help. How much do we love our own Chapter and the Order of the Eastern Star?

What better way can we show our love than by working at keeping these solemn and sincere promises?

In so doing we can always turn to the teaching of Electa and know as we practice loving one another we will also be practicing the keeping of our OBLIGATION. To express our love and our respect for our beloved Order we must constantly remember that when we took this Obligation we entered upon a new phase of life, and that now we are numbered among the members of this Order who have for our inspiration the Star of Bethlehem, and that so long as we keep close to God and His teachings, we may confidently believe that we will come safely to the end of our journey.

Your life and mine should be richer and fuller since we took our OBLIGATION in the Order of the Eastern Star.

☆ ☆ ☆ ☆ ☆

8. OUR UNSPOKEN OBLIGATIONS
By MARGARET MELISSINOS (*New York*)

What is our obligation as members of the Order of the Eastern Star? What is required of us? What do we have to do to remain members in good standing? What is our purpose and why do we exist?

We seldom give much thought to these questions except in terms of paying our dues on time, attending our meetings as regularly as possible, supporting our Chapter and its projects, aiding our sisters and brothers in distress. Yes—these are our obligations—obvious and apparent.

But what of the obligations which are *not written down*, obligations which are not sworn to verbally?

When we accept membership in an altruistic movement, we are, to begin with, aspirants of a loftier way of thinking and behaving. Unconsciously, we are seeking association with others of like ideals and principles. This is man's, and woman's, inherent desire to lift himself to a higher spiritual understanding. These aspirations place restrictions on us which become moral obligations to ourselves and to others. Our patterns of behavior must follow the strict dictates of a clear conscience. The virtues of love, trust, and honor are our constant companions. Kindness, sympathetic understanding, and tolerance are our direct responsibility to others.

Suspicion, distrust, gossip, maliciousness, and vindictiveness are behavior faults of the unenlightened. It is our unspoken obligation to turn our backs on such behavior.

As Eastern Stars, the symbol of all that is pure and good is constantly before us. A love that has endured for centuries is held out to us as a beacon to follow.

When we allow our consciences to follow the Golden Rule, and live our lives in and out of the Chapter so that none can reproach, we are fulfilling all of our obligations as members of the Order of the Eastern Star; as children of a kind and just God, and as worthwhile contributors to a better world.

We will find that our prayerful moments in the Chapter session are sincere and uplifting experiences.

The good feeling within ourselves, the sense of doing what is right, the feeling of love and charity to our neighbors, all contribute to a feeling of well-being—emotionally, spiritually, and physically, and our reward is from the bread that has been cast upon the waters.

☆   ☆   ☆   ☆   ☆

125

9. WORTHY MATRON'S ADDRESS TO MASTER MASONS

WE are happy to acknowledge the debt of gratitude we owe to Masonry for the brother whose relationship gave us the privilege of petitioning our beloved Order. We are proud of the fact that we are the wives, daughters, mothers, widows and sisters of Master Masons.

We of the Eastern Star sisterhood pay homage to the one who, by the sweat of his brow, provides us a comfortable home, many luxuries as well as necessities, and is entitled to be the head of the household. We are ever mindful of his right to a position of honor in the community and we stand ready to make sacrifices to attain that end.

By example we teach in our homes the command, "honor thy father and thy mother," and endeavor to so live that by thought, word and deed we will impress the youth in our homes with the truth that an upright life is beyond all price and that we have faith in the one whose name we bear; faith in his motives, faith in his judgment, and faith that he has our best good at heart.

We often remind ourselves that the Order of the Eastern Star does not claim to be a part of the Masonic Fraternity, yet as the wives, daughters, mothers, widows and sisters of Masons we are tremendously interested in the ideals and aspirations which you cherish.

We owe our inception as an Order to a Master Mason and we are dependent upon the growth of your Order for our own growth. We welcome Master Masons as members of our Order and we rely upon a Mason's aid and counsel in the East. And to the Masonic Fraternity we pledge the earnest and interested support of their womankind.

☆ ☆ ☆ ☆ ☆

10. WELCOME TO PAST MATRONS AND PAST PATRONS

DEAR toilers in our beautiful garden, we welcome you;
Upon your breast you wear a badge of service true.
You were welcomed yesterday, you'll be welcomed
tomorrow,
But no warmer welcome greets you than the one to
follow.

Builders of yesterday, you have stood the test of years;
You toiled through sunshine, and sometimes through
tears.
But you builded well and strong for our loved Eastern
Star
And the work you have done has carried our Chapter
far.

There's courage and help in the ring of your voice, the
clasp of your hand;
In the warmth of your smile, so friendly and true.
Dear sisters and brothers, we treasure these greetings
from your faithful band;
And the warmest of welcomes I'm extending to you.

☆   ☆   ☆   ☆   ☆

11. PAST MATRONS' AND PAST PATRONS' RESPONSE TO WELCOME

By the courtesy of our Worthy Matron, it is my privilege and very great pleasure, in behalf of the Past Matrons and Past Patrons of our Chapter, to respond to these gracious words of welcome, so beautifully expressed.

We do appreciate with all our hearts the nice things you have so generously accredited to us. If we have been builders, if we have provided a stepping stone upward for a fellow being, then our work has not been in vain.

As Past Matrons and Past Patrons, we are the servants of our Chapter and our Beloved Order. Though the day of our administration in the East is passed, we are ever ready to respond to calls for service.

We will always strive to strengthen the ties of friendship, promote the prosperity of our Order, and protect its unity, integrity and strength by maintaining the truest fraternal spirit.

We heartily rejoice with you, dear Worthy Matron, and we congratulate the Chapter upon a most successful administration, one which adds the lustre of a treasured page in the history of our Chapter.

☆   ☆   ☆   ☆   ☆

12. FAREWELL TRIBUTE TO WORTHY MATRON

Just a short year ago we expressed our felicitations and warm good wishes upon your attaining the East as the presiding officer of our Chapter, and now we rejoice with you upon your year of accomplishments.

We have been told that it is idle to be a "dreamer of dreams," and yet it is the dreams and aspirations of yesterday which, put into action today, will make the history of the future.

Should you feel that your ambitions have exceeded your accomplishments, may you recall these lines of the poet—

> There are hills too steep for our feet to climb
> There are goals too far to gain;
> In every dreamer's breast there's a glorious best,
> That he may never attain.
> For the poet dies with his song unsung,
> The artist at last grows faint,
> And he sinks to sleep and the grave must keep
> The picture he had planned to paint.
>
> Oh, we never do reach our fullest height,
> And we never do our all;
> We must turn away at the close of day
> When the tools from our fingers fall.
> But it is not failure to hold a dream
> That never on earth comes true;
> For the tasks of earth that we miss on earth
> Are left for our souls to do.

☆　☆　☆　☆　☆

13. MATRON'S FAREWELL ADDRESS

Dear Sisters and Brothers:

The past year has seemed like unto a day. Bright hopes and happy anticipations appeared in its rosy dawn. Then came hours of work and the noonday passed. The afternoon came on apace, with more duties. Now the sunset is here, with its many realizations and memories, and as the twilight shadows deepen I whisper this benediction to you:

> God bless you, is my wish,
> O friends of mine;
> May roses bloom along the way,
> O friends of mine;
> May your every wish come true,
> May joy and plenty come to you,
> And victory crown whate'er you do,
> O friends of mine.

A year ago, I seemed to be standing in a valley of much promise, o'ershadowed with a mountain whose summit I must reach. I recall days with problems and opportunities, days with sunshine and days with shadow.

Today I thank God for the view from the summit— that I can look down the ever winding pathway and recall the brook gladdened meadows, made golden by the bright rays of Star fellowship.

Grateful am I for the hills that seemed hard and steep and high, for the streams I had to cross. The struggle gave me strength and courage to enjoy the flowers along the way, the understanding to appreciate

131

the hand that helped, the words of cheer and love, and the inspiration of our Star in the East, guiding my footsteps ever onward.

With gratitude for the past and an earnest prayer for the future, that God's richest blessings may ever rest upon you, I bid you farewell.

☆　☆　☆　☆　☆

14. PATRON'S FAREWELL ADDRESS

THIS evening marks the close of another Eastern Star year and it is well to reflect on what it has brought to our Chapter and our Order. A year nearer—to what? A year further—from what? A year richer—in what?

Happily we are privileged to report a year nearer a universal allegiance to our principles, further from misconceptions, richer in the achievement of our purpose.

These achievements have been of substantial character. Our Order's success is built upon the firmest of all foundations—that of practical idealism. The Eastern Star is not a spinner of theoretical cobwebs or a weaver of impossible fancies. In every field of its endeavors it has been efficient and successful. In the direction of development, our aim has been for strength, stability, and lofty purpose, rather than numerical growth.

By this yardstick of measurement, I believe this year has been satisfactory. We enjoy a pleasing past, a calm present, an inviting future. The past provides principles and policies for purposeful undertakings. With these as our guide, the present has made marked progress along the highway of creditable accomplishments.

The record of my term of office is before you. If any good has been accomplished, I shall be satisfied and need no praise. If there have been failures, I know you will understand that they do not come from lack of interest or effort and that your generous natures will overlook the failures and magnify the good.

And now, as I step down and take my place with the Past Patrons of our Chapter, I pledge my hearty

133

and understanding support to my successor. Brother
_____, may your labors and your honors
throughout your year bring you as much satisfaction
and joy as my year has to me.

☆ ☆ ☆ ☆ ☆

17. CEREMONIES

1. Installation
2. Addendum Honoring Star Points
3. Star Point Ceremony
4. Do you Remember? An Obligation Ceremony
5. Obligation Night
6. The Shining Gateway. A Necrology Ceremony
7. Safe Home from Orbit. To Welcome Home Deputy or Lecturer
8. District Deputy Night
9. What Is a Mason?
10. This is Your Life, Ima Star, Past Matron
11. What is a Patron? Honoring Past Patrons
12. Addendum Honoring Past Matrons
13. A Thought for Past Matrons Night
14. Short Ceremony Honoring Past Matrons and Patrons
15. Christmas
16. Sittin' and Rockin'—To Honor Retiring Matron and Patron
17. To Honor Retiring Matron whose Husband is Patron
18. Fathers Day Ceremony. For any Young Girls Group

☆　☆　☆　☆　☆

1. INSTALLATION CEREMONY WITH PRESENTATION OF FLOWERS AND STAR POINT EMBLEMS INTO THEIR KEEPING

(To be Given by Past Matrons)

By VEE HANSEN LOHMANN, P.M. (N.Y.)

The Jr. Past Matron is the first speaker; other speakers who approach the Star Points may be Past Matrons or other members. Each should have one or more flowers of the Star Point color to present to the Star Point she addresses, as well as the Station Emblem which she will give into the keeping of the Star Point by placing such on the pedestal.

Jr. Past Matron should have a five-color bouquet and a boutonniere which she will present to the W.M. and W.P. Past Matrons, at proper time for the ceremony, should rise from their seats on the side lines and approach the Star Point. After speaking and presenting flowers and placing the emblem on the pedestal, she should stand beside the Star Point she has addressed until the entire ceremony is completed. When the Star Point is addressed, she should stand.

Jr. Past Matron, carrying the bonquet and boutonniere, walks to the East and stands at foot of dais, facing the altar. She remains in this position until all have spoken.

JR. P.M.:

In the center of our Chapter room, where all may see, stands the altar. It is an altar firm and strong and upon it we place our Holy Bible. It is the place we kneel and

136

pledge our lives to God, to practice charity, truth and loving kindness. It is the place from which we draw strength and inspiration, joy and comfort. It is a place that sends out rays of light to the five Points of our Star whose lessons we all must heed.

1ST P.M. (*approaches Adah, who rises*):

Sister Adah, the BLUE ray emanating from our altar light sends out a lesson on the integrity of Jephthah's daughter. This lesson you will teach to others. Your Chapter, through me, gives you these blue flowers which are symbolic of truth and filial devotion. I now place your emblem of office—the Sword and Veil—on the pedestal at your station.

2ND P.M. (*approaches Ruth, who rises*):

Sister Ruth, our altar light sends out a YELLOW ray, emblematic of those virtues of loyalty and industry which you will be expected to relate. These yellow flowers which are given to you will remind you of those attributes so necessary to all. I now place the emblem of your office—the Sheaf of Wheat—on the pedestal at your station.

3RD P.M. (*approaches Esther, who rises*):

Sister Esther, a pure WHITE ray beams from our altar light. Its lessons tell of courage, of justice. These lessons will be explained by you. There is no more

137

beautiful a flower than the white lily which denotes purity and these white flowers we now give to you. I place on the pedestal at your station the emblems of your office—the Crown and Scepter.

4TH P.M. (*approaches Martha, who rises*):

Sister Martha, shining from our altar light is a beautiful GREEN ray. Green, in its beauty, signifies life, and hope. You will be instructing us in faith, the faith of Martha which sustained her when she had lost a loved brother. Accept these flowers as an expression of your Chapter's faith in you. I now place on the pedestal at your station the emblem of your office—the Broken Column.

5TH P.M. (*approaches Electa, who rises*):

Sister Electa, there is a vivid clear RED ray coming from our altar light and beaming straight to you. Red has always stood for fortitude and steadfastness—and these beautiful red roses from your Chapter denote love and kindness, virtues exemplified by Electa which you will explain in the lessons you teach. I now place on the pedestal at your station the emblem of your office—the Cup.

JR. P.M.:

Our altar light is a shining place and has sent its beams in the spectrum hues to the five Points of our Star who have been chosen to inspire us all with their lessons. (*Turns and faces the East.*)

Worthy Matron, this sacred altar, our Holy Bible, this station in the East, the members—all are now in your keeping. The meaning of these flowers I know you well understand. Please accept them from your Chapter with our love and our pledge for cooperation in the months ahead.

Worthy Patron, I give you flowers, too—four bright ones and a white one and their significance you well know. Your Chapter also wants you to know that we hold you in high esteem and this is our way of telling you so.

☆   ☆   ☆   ☆   ☆

2. ADDENDUM HONORING NEWLY INSTALLED STAR POINTS

By FAY MAY, P.M. (*Ohio*)

My sisters, as you portray the Heroines of our Order, may you exemplify their virtues in your lives.

Sister Adah, you will give us instruction in fidelity. May you be blessed with firm convictions and deep understanding.

Sister Ruth, you will teach us of constancy. May you be blessed with patience and confidence.

Sister Esther, we will hear your lesson of loyalty. May you be blessed with the dear ties of family and friends.

Sister Martha, yours will be words of faith. May you be blessed with strength of heart and peace of mind.

Sister Electa, you will remind us of love. May you be blessed with a fervent devotion to all mankind.

So, my sisters, may your service to us bring blessings to you.

☆　　☆　　☆　　☆　　☆

3. A SHORT STAR POINT CEREMONY

Presenting Flowers or Ribbons

By Margaret J. Burns, P.M. (*Missouri*)

Properties needed: A flower basket filled with flowers (or ribbons) in the emblematic colors should be waiting beside Marshal's chair. If ribbons are used, Speaker should substitute "ribbon" for "blossom," "flower," "garland" and "cluster."

Speaker: the Marshal.

Directions: When directed by the Worthy Matron, the Marshal shall step forward from her station and bow to the Star Points who shall then rise. All may remain in these positions, or may slowly assemble near the altar. If the latter, then the Star Points shall step slowly backward to their stations following the Marshal's address to Electa, the Marshal stopping mid-way to her station.

The Marshal shall hold the appropriate flower (or ribbon) before her while addressing each Point, handing it to her before proceeding to the next Point. Following her final address to the Points, she shall bow to seat them, then step slowly backward to her station, bow to the Worthy Matron and be seated.

Marshal:

You soon soon shall speak of our lovely queens, so
    noble, brave and true,
With their colors bright—red and green and white,
Purest gold and royal blue;

141

How dearly we hold these queens of old, who heard
    the Master's call,
And among the lovely thousands, fairest of them all!

(*To Adah*)

This blossom (or ribbon) of blue shall speak for you
    of a daughter's faithful love,
Of her father's humility before such fidelity,
To honor and God above.

(*To Ruth*)

This flower (or ribbon) of gold shall a story unfold of
    a widow's deep distress,
'Twill tell of her gleaming from dawn until evening
And to her constancy attest.

(*To Esther*)

This garland (or ribbon) of white, this spotless white,
    shall speak of a royal queen,
Of her courage and beauty; of her daring in duty
And of her loyalty serene.

(*To Martha*)

In this cluster (or ribbon) of green, a lesson is seen of
    a sister's grief and pain,
Of her faith when she said, "Tho' my brother be dead,
I know he shall live again."

CEREMONIES

(To Electa)

This beauty (or ribbon) of red shall a radiance shed
    like the deeds of the valiant mother,
With the cross on her breast, she with fervency
    expressed:
"Let us all love one another."

(To ALL)

These garlands of glory all tell the glad story, no
    sorrow nor grief can bedim;
Like the Wise Men afar, we have seen the bright star
And have come to worship Him.

☆   ☆   ☆   ☆   ☆

4. DO YOU REMEMBER?
An Obligation Ceremony
(With Adoptation if it is also the Chapter Birthday)

By MARGARET MELISSINOS (*New York*)

Miniature Bibles given to all to hold will make the ceremony more effective. Star Points will kneel at altar in correct position. Spotlight turned on the altar. Speaking parts may be taken by one person who is an especially good speaker, or by various officers as in the adaptation for Birthday Night.

WORTHY MATRON:

My sisters and brothers, tonight has been designated as OBLIGATION NIGHT. We, who seek membership in this Order, are asked to take this obligation so that we may be more conscious of our duties to God, our Order, and our fraternal brothers and sisters. It is more than an obligation; it is a sacred vow and God is our witness.

Sisters Conductress and Associate Conductress, will you give every one in the room a miniature Bible so that we may each hold this as we proceed with the ceremony.

(Soft music while Conductresses pass out the little Bibles)

As we hold His Bible in our hands and promise secrecy and obedience, aid, sympathy, truth and loyalty, we are reminded that malice, envy, revenge, and selfishness have no part in the life of an Eastern Star member. I am sure that no one, however frivolous she may be,

144

has ever assumed this obligation lightly, but we are all apt to forget, at times, the beauty and import of the words and the true meaning of our promises. Let us go back to that memorable day when each of us knelt at the altar for the very first time.

Worthy Patron, will you proceed with the Obligation Ceremony?

WORTHY PATRON:

Will the sisters representing the Five Heroines of our Order represent each member here by kneeling at the altar as the candidate does.

(Star Points take positions at altar in correct order, each holding a candidate size Bible. The Bibles should have been previously placed on the altar.)

ELECTA   (altar)   ADAH

MARTHA — ESTHER — RUTH

(Warder turns down lights with spot on altar. SOFT MUSIC while Speaker walks to WEST between prep. room door and A.M. Soft music also as she walks from one position to another.)

SPEAKER *(in the west)*:

Do you remember the night you entered the preparation room door, and the things that filled your heart and mind at that time?

(walks to Cond. station)

Do you recall the gentle guidance of your Conductress as she graciously led you around the room with words of encouragement and enlightenment?

(walks and stands behind ADAH at altar)

145

Do you remember the story of Adah—and the sacrifice she made for her father? Think deeply of her virtues— FILIAL DEVOTION, INTEGRITY and TRUTH.

(steps behind RUTH at altar)

Do you remember the story of Ruth—and her trials as she journeyed with her mother-in-law? Think deeply of her virtues—CONSTANCY, LOYALTY and INDUS- TRY.

(steps behind ESTHER at altar)

Do you recall the story of Queen Esther, who bravely faced death in her concern for the welfare of her people? Meditate on her virtues—JUSTICE, COUR- AGE and FIDELITY.

(steps behind MARTHA at altar)

Do you remember the faith of Martha, and her sin- cere belief in the infallibility and love of the Lord? Dwell upon her virtue—ABIDING FAITH—and hold it close to your heart.

(steps behind ELECTA at altar)

Remember the story of Electa and the price she paid for refusing to renounce her faith. Think deeply of her virtues—BENEFICENCE, FORTITUDE and STEAD- FASTNESS, for they offer great strength in times of stress.

(Speaker remains standing behind Electa)

WORTHY PATRON:

Will the members please assemble around the altar and place their hands as though taking the obligation at the altar, and repeat after me.

(Patron and Matron step down as do Sec'y and Treas. Patron steps to altar)

— OBLIGATION GIVEN —

(Worthy Patron directs Star Points to rise after obligation)

CHAPLAIN *(who will have taken a place in the circle close to west of altar, without instruction, kneels for the following prayer)*:

Eternal Father, bear witness to the oaths of our sisters and brothers, as they are offered reverently and honestly in Thy presence. Help each of us to live our lives exemplifying the virtues of the Five Heroines of our Order, and direct our efforts and endeavors in the path of Light and Truth. Amen. *(rises)*

ALL: "Blest be the Tie that Binds."

☆   ☆   ☆   ☆   ☆

ADAPTATION IF IT IS ALSO CHAPTER BIRTHDAY

WORTHY MATRON:

Tonight we say Happy Birthday to _____ Chapter. We can think of no better way to extend our sincere good wishes than to rededicate ourselves openly to the Chapter and to the Order by reaffirming our devotion in the renewal of our obligation.

ASSOCIATE MATRON: Do you remember the night you entered the preparation room door, and the things that filled your heart and mind at that time?

CONDUCTRESS: Do you recall the gentle guidance of your Conductress as she graciously led you around the room with words of encouragement and enlightenment?

147

ADAH: Do you remember my story, the story of Adah, and the sacrifice I made for my father? Think deeply of my virtues—FILIAL DEVOTION, INTEGRITY and TRUTH.

RUTH: Do you remember my story, the Story of Ruth, and my trials as I journeyed with my mother-in-law? Think deeply of my virtues—CONSTANCY, LOYALTY and INDUSTRY.

ESTHER: Do you recall my story, Queen Esther, who bravely faced death in my concern for the welfare of my people? Meditate on my virtues—JUSTICE, COURAGE and FIDELITY.

MARTHA: Do you remember my story, the Faith of Martha, and my sincere belief in the infallibility and love of my Lord? Dwell upon my virtue—ABIDING FAITH—and hold it close to your heart.

ELECTA: I am Electa. Remember my story, and the price I paid for refusing to renounce my faith. Think deeply of my virtues—BENEFICENCE, FORTITUDE and STEADFASTNESS, for they offer great strength in times of stress.

(*Marshals escort Matron, Patron, A. Matron and Patron, Treas. and Sec'y down to the floor. PATRON stands at the East and gives the obligation and the entire room responds. Officers are then escorted back to their stations and CHAPLAIN goes to altar and kneels giving the prayer as in first section. All join in singing "Blest be the Tie that Binds.*")

☆　☆　☆　☆　☆

5. OBLIGATION NIGHT

By ELEANOR B. WESSNER, P.M. (*Minnesota*)

*Those taking part: W.M., W.P., Chaplain, A.M.,
Cond. and A.C. Conductresses stand near altar in front
of their stations. Chap. takes her position at the Bible.
A.M. stands west of altar behind Chaplain. W.M.
raises the Chapter before she and W.P. step down in
front of altar facing west. All except W.P. light candles
as obligation is given.*

WORTHY MATRON: (*when all are in position*):
    Let's renew our obligation
    To the Star that we all love,
    Give our Order our attention
    With the help of God above.

ASSOCIATE MATRON:
    Our sacred vows again we pledge
    To do all within our power;
    Once again we ask for courage
    For this and every hour.

CONDUCTRESSES (*in unison while all light candles*):
    These little candles we here light
    Denote that our Star shines bright;
    With Faith and Love in heart
    Rededicate ourselves before we part.

WORTHY PATRON: (*gives Obligation and all repeat*)

CHAPLAIN:
    Lord, we ask Thy aid,
    Teach our members gathered here

To remember all the promises they made
And to keep them all forever dear. AMEN.

(Officers all join hands around altar and repeat in unison):

Here we are at the altar
Pledging our good faith to keep,
We promise never to falter,
Blessings on us our Good Lord will heap.

☆　☆　☆　☆　☆

6. THE SHINING GATEWAY

A Necrology Ceremony
By MARGARET J. BURNS, P.M. *(Missouri)*

Properties: A white or gold swinging gate in front of the dais. Baskets or urns of flowers or trailing vines may be added on either side.

Speaker: Chairman of Necrology Committee. When the W.M. calls for the report of the Necrology Committee, the Chairman shall advance to the East, stopping at the right of Marshal's station. She addresses the first paragraph of the service to the W.M., then turns and faces the Chapter for the remainder. If desired, other members of the Committee may enter with the Chairman and speak parts of the ceremony.

Worthy Matron, your Necrology Committee appreciates the honor of presenting this ceremony in loving memory of those of our Order, and their loved ones, who have passed through the Shining Gateway of Death this year. It is indeed appropriate that we consider the journey we all sooner or later shall make and to envision that glorious land where we shall forever dwell with Him, Who alone giveth life—both earthly and eternal.

Memory is one of heaven's richest gifts. But far transcending it in glory is the priceless endowment of *faith*. United, they form the basis for our contemplation tonight.

"In the midst of life we are in death, yet, in the very presence of death, we glimpse eternal life." Girded by faith we fearlessly meet that pallid gaze, for looming

151

bright beyond his gloomy presence, we glimpse the roseate promise of heaven. The earthly life that may have seemed a futile quest, never to be rewarded, is transformed by faith into a triumphant adventure and we travel cheerfully toward that beckoning glow. Faith assures us that, after passing through death's Shining Gateway, the grateful traveler will join a celestial chorus whose songs of praise shall never end and clasp the nail-scarred hand of Him Who said "Come unto Me and I will give you rest."

In loving memory of _____ (*Grand Officers of Grand Chapter*) of _____, we dedicate this immortal hymn.

SOLOIST: (*one verse of "In the Garden," or other appropriate hymn*)

The mystic call of death is imperative and not to be denied, yet, this ghostly visitor comes not empty-handed. The very inevitability of his arrival provides impetus to our earthly life by enriching the depth of its meaning, and by giving urgency to its purpose. When his chilling hand touches the Shining Gateway it also reveals the glories which lie in that haven beyond—the welcoming arms of His love and the tortured feet at which the traveler lays his burdens down.

The relentless wheels of time roll on, silently, but surely bringing us to that Shining Gateway. How vainly in life we try to peer beyond its portals! How vainly we strive to penetrate its sheltered mysteries! But not until that Gateway swings wide for us shall we know the splendors awaiting our eager eyes. Until that blessed day arrives, we shall be unwavering in faith and zealous in our labors, ever finding comfort in the precious memories we cherish.

We would recall those who sought and received the privilege of fellowship in our Order; who labored diligently in our midst; who blessed us with the radiance of their spirits and left us desolate by their departure. By these welling memories, let us be inspired to exemplify in our own lives the virtues of Loyalty, Constancy, Fidelity, Faith and Love which characterized theirs.

> At journey's end, a Shining Gate swings ever wide
> and free
> When twilight nears, a trumpet clear will call for
> you and me.
> We'll find beyond that Gateway, deep in the
> timeless West,
> A home so fair with Him to share—sweet gift of
> peace and rest.

With this melodic tribute, we pay homage to the memory of _____ (*Past Matrons and Patrons and other officers of Chapter*).

SOLOIST: (*one verse of "Lead Kindly Light"*)

To the unbeliever, death is a blind leap into the perilous dark; the promise of eternal life, a bewildering fantasy. The believer is sustained by the unfaltering trust that eternal life is a glorious reality—the gracious gift of God through faith in His Son, Jesus Christ.

The spirit is undaunted by death because it is returning to the Father Who gave it. Taking the Father's hand through life will lead us fearlessly through the gateway of death. It is not a blind leap into the dark; not a journey into a far and unknown country, but simply the soul's change of residence. Challenging though it is, the hand of death cannot impede the spirit's upward surge, nor divert its instinctive flight to the Father Who gave it. The unerring hand of Him Who guided through the labyrinth of life, will lead triumphantly through the portals of death.

Death is slumber to the weary, surcease to tempest-
    torn,
A shelter warm, endearing—sweet peace from
    clanging storm.

In memory of those members of our Chapter who clasped that guiding hand in life and were sustained by it in death, we offer this bouquet of song.

SOLOIST: *(one verse of "Beautiful Isle of Somewhere")*

What is it that sometimes speaks to the heart so clearly as immortality draws nigh? Is it the soul's inherent desire to return to its Creator? What is it that can gently replace trembling apprehension with towering assurance? It is that sublime gift of trustful *faith* with which our Blessed Redeemer has satisfied the desires of our hearts, enriched the days of our life and enlarged the scope of our horizons.

The forlorn spirit of the unbeliever looks up with anguished eyes as he contemplates the fathomless void he calls death, but the soul of the Christian rests in the sweet certainty that heaven is near.

> How sweet it is to rest in peace upon the Master's breast
> When all our toiling days have ceased, and pain is lulled to rest.

With this song we hold in sacred memory the loved ones of our Chapter members who have entered the Shining Gateway this year.

SOLOIST: (*one verse of "Blest be the Tie that Binds"*)

What lies beyond the Shining Gate we cannot tell, but our *faith* gives us a calm assurance that beyond the gate we shall see the Promised Land.

CHAPLAIN:

Our Father, we adore Thy Holy Name; we praise Thee for the unsearchable riches of Thy love and grace; we thank Thee for the gift of Life and for the ever-open Gateway Thou has provided. To Thee, by whose death itself has been swallowed up in victory, we give humble thanks for the lives and influence of those who have been commemorated in this service. In the Name of Thy Son, we pray for a joyous reunion beyond that Shining Gateway where we shall forever share the glory of Thy presence. Amen.

ORGANIST: (*softly plays Dvorak's "Largo"* [*Going Home*])

☆   ☆   ☆   ☆   ☆

7. SAFE HOME FROM ORBIT

Presentation for Returning Deputy or Lecturer
By F. BEATRICE MACINTYRE

Properties needed: TV. Perhaps your decorations could include a cardboard "capsule" or small space ships strung near the East. If a gift is presented, that same idea could be carried out.

Five speaking parts are all short. Four to eight additional people could enter and be part of "crowd."

At a signal from the presiding officer, those taking part enter and gather about the TV. One turns to the station excitedly while the others watch. Some look upward at the "sky." The Guest, or Guests of Honor should have been escorted to the East.

1ST SPEAKER:

What in the world are you looking for?
Don't say we are approaching another war!

2ND SPEAKER:

Where have you been hiding all this day?
Our astronauts are on their way.

3RD SPEAKER:

Once again, we've beaten the Reds;
Brought confusion on their heads.
Two in orbit our District sent;
They've functioned beautifully
Since they went.

4TH SPEAKER:

The reason our _____ (*Chapter, Court, etc.*) is feeling gay

'Tis _____ _____ we laud today.
Her (*his*) work in the _____, success has
     brought;
We're proud indeed of the job she's (*he's*) wrought!

1ST SPEAKER:

Look! from the capsule, our _____ comes,
Unruffled by the feat.
Successfully, their orbit ends,
Our _____ (*Chapter, Court, etc.*) again to
     greet.

3RD SPEAKER:

You have served us well;
You've soared to noble heights;
The orbit has been perfect,
And we're glad you're back tonight.

4TH SPEAKER:

Welcome _____ _____,
We're glad you've done so well;
We're proud of your representation;
Your work has been really swell!

2ND SPEAKER:

Yes, our _____ (*Chapter, Court, etc.*) is
     happy, Welcome _____
Back with us tonight.
You've shown the stars along the way
A splendid orbital flight.

CONDUCTRESS (*presents gift*):

Sincerely, our _____ is grateful for the
     way you've flown;

Your work has been exemplary;
Our prestige has certainly grown!
As a token of our true esteem
This gift we give to you—
Hoping you will realize
Our gratitude to you.

(*If a gift is also to be given the Lecturer, use the following*):

To you, _____ _____, who journeyed
Beside our _____ _____, fair,
We thank you for your helpfulness;
So glad that you were there.
We're grateful, too, you're safely down
From the District's outstanding trip—
Happily you did your part
In the landing of this ship.

May happiness attend you both,
And memories, fine, remain
Of all the bright success you've had—
WELCOME HOME (or here) again!

NOTE: *This, with few changes, can be used to welcome home the Lecturer and above addressed to the Deputy.*

☆   ☆   ☆   ☆   ☆

8. DISTRICT DEPUTY NIGHT

By MARGARET MELISSINOS (N.Y.)

WORTHY MATRON:

Right Worthy Sister _____ and Right Worthy Brother _____, as sisters and brothers, and as very dear friends, we welcome you most cordially on your official visit to our Chapter.

We applaud your appointment as guardians of the Path of Truth, and we know that you will execute your entrusted duties with dignity and dedication. The lamp of knowledge which lights our Path expresses an eloquent message in each ray. Listen—

ADAH:

The BLUE ray speaks of integrity and devotion. The same virtues that motivated Adah's dedication to filial servitude, inspired you toward fraternal service in the Path of Truth.

RUTH:

My YELLOW ray speaks of constancy. The industrious loyalty of Ruth to her mother-in-law matches your own constant perseverance in the pursuit of unselfish service to your sisters and brothers.

ESTHER.

The WHITE ray of Esther shines brightly with courage. Fidelity in the pursuit of justice can only be maintained by a brave heart and a dedicated soul. These virtues walk hand in hand with service, a moral goodness that you both so sincerely exemplify.

MARTHA:

Martha's GREEN ray of abiding faith shines as a

159

beacon from the lamp of knowledge. Certainly its warmth has filled your hearts with the virtue that sustains and nourishes our beings. Faith in your beliefs must have guided your footsteps in the direction you have taken.

ELECTA:

The RED ray reaches out in warmth and devotion. Love is a virtue that finds its own reward, and in our love for one another, our inner beings are elevated and inspired toward even greater heights. Your own upward path is silent proof of this truth.

WORTHY PATRON:

Right Worthy Sister _____ and Right Worthy Brother _____ the rays of our Eastern Star glow with many virtues, yet all are made brighter by one quality—SERVICE. Each of our heroines gave of herself to someone or something. What nobler path than to serve our sisters and brothers in leadership?

(*Chaplain approaches Altar and kneels*)

CHAPLAIN:

Heavenly Father, bless our leaders and protect the path of service they would travel. Let there be joy and satisfaction beyond each hill, and peace and contentment upon the completion of their journey. Amen.

☆　　☆　　☆　　☆　　☆

9. WHAT IS A MASON?

A Master Masons Night Ceremony

By MARGARET MELISSINOS (*New York*)

WORTHY MATRON:

Worthy Patron, sisters and brothers, we wish to extend a very hearty welcome to all our brothers on this long-anticipated occasion, and we sincerely hope you will enjoy our offering.

WORTHY PATRON:

"What is a Mason?" A MASON is a MAN and a BROTHER whose TRUST is in GOD. He meets you on the LEVEL and acts upon the SQUARE. TRUTH is his COMPASS and he is ever PLUMB. He has a true GRIP on all that is RITE. He is loyal to his ORDER and whatever his DEGREE, he is MASTER of himself. In the LODGE of Life, he wears unstained the white LAMBSKIN of Innocence. From his INITIATION as an ENTERED APPRENTICE, he travels ever EAST toward the LIGHT OF WISDOM until he receives the final—the DIVINE PASSWORD that admits him into the INEFFABLE PRESENCE OF THE ETERNAL SUPREME GRAND MASTER OF THE UNIVERSE—GOD.

WORTHY MATRON:

Sisters and brothers, you have heard our brother deliver a very beautiful rendition of "What Is A Mason?" As Eastern Stars, we would like to offer our own interpretation of "What Is A Mason?"

161

1ST SPEAKER:

A Mason is a husband, who one evening took a walk
And he joined some other fellows who gave HIM a
chance to talk.

2ND SPEAKER:

And he liked the friendly gatherings where the
women weren't allowed;
And he found his brand new stature made him
masculinely proud.

3RD SPEAKER:

He attended all the meetings, and he went out more
and more
'Til the dates upon the calendar got the little woman
sore.

4TH SPEAKER:

So he talked with all the fellows and he learned his
marriage strife
Was a very common problem—what to do with good
friend wife!

5TH SPEAKER:

So the brothers huddled closer and their brains began
to whirl—
What would soothe the ruffled feathers of the little,
at-home girl?

6TH SPEAKER:

Then one Masonic wit beamed, "We can't lose our
poker games—

Let us form a female order for the troubled little
dames."

7TH SPEAKER:

"What's the harm in women meeting? They can have
themselves a ball.
There the hens can cluck and clatter all around the
temple hall."

8TH SPEAKER:

So the Eastern Star was founded. But the boys did
err, my friends,
When they wrote in regulations that a Mason must
attend.

9TH SPEAKER:

But the ladies were delighted with a man around the
place;
And they flocked to every meeting just to see his
handsome face.

10TH SPEAKER:

Then one spider in the female web said, "If one man
is so nice,
Wouldn't Masons to the rafters be much more than
twice as nice?"
So the clever gals united, and the men with all their
might
Were drawn meekly to the spider web—on MASTER
MASONS NIGHT!

ASSOCIATE PATRON (*hurries to the East and raises his hand for attention, turning to Matron and Patron*):
For the defense, for the defense, Your Honor,
You can always tell a Mason at collations when you feed him—
But a Mason is a brother when you really, really need him!
(*returns to his seat*)

SOLOIST (*to tune of "I'll Get By"*):

We will be, as long as we have you
Though we may seem to stand alone, all on our own, it isn't true;
Let's avow fraternal love anew,
In harmony, with Masonry, we'll always be, with you.

☆   ☆   ☆   ☆   ☆

10. THIS IS YOUR LIFE, IMA STAR, PAST MATRON

A Humorous Skit Honoring Past Matrons or the Retiring Matron

By FAY MAY, P.M. (*Ohio*)

Characters: Narrator and one actress to do the pantomimes, an organist or pianist. The pantomimist should walk back and forth across the room, or stage, so that all may see. She may add to the suggestions any actions that are natural.

NARRATOR:

Tonight we proudly present the thrilling, true-life story of a Past Matron. This is Your Life, Ima Star. You, Ima Star, were initiated into Watta Chapter. You were so impressed with it all that you proudly displayed your membership pin on every outfit.

(*Ima wears a very large, shiny star. MUSIC: "Twinkle, Twinkle, Little Star"*)

NARRATOR:

Anxious to be a real part of the Order, you, Ima Star, cheerfully accepted a position on a very important committee.

(*Ima dries dishes. MUSIC: "I've Been Workin' on the Railroad"*)

NARRATOR:

Soon your talents are discovered and you, Ima Star, are promoted to the officers' ranks.

(*Ima carries large sheaf. MUSIC: any march*)

NARRATOR:

And now, congratulations, Ima Star! You are elected

Associate Conductress and eagerly begin your trip to the East.

(*Ima carries luggage and waves. MUSIC: "Sentimental Journey"*)

NARRATOR:

As Conductress, you, Ima Star, become a serious student of ritual and protocol.

(*Ima reads big book with large glasses. MUSIC: "School Days"*)

NARRATOR:

Ima Star, Associate Matron, busy with present duties, you still must find time to plan for the future.

(*Ima consults crystal ball. MUSIC: "Beyond the Blue Horizon"*)

NARRATOR:

At last, you, Ima Star, are the Worthy Matron of Watta Chapter. Your dreams come true. You preside.

(*Ima wields huge hammer. MUSIC: "Anvil Chorus"*)

NARRATOR:

Soon you are Ima Star, Past Matron. With mixed emotions you put down the gavel and head for the easy chair. But, not so fast, Ima. Your chapter needs you still. Your telephone rings and your replies are ready. You will still work wherever needed.

(*Ima dries dishes as before. MUSIC: "I've Been Workin' on the Railroad"*)

NARRATOR:

The circle's completed, but your work will never be done. You'll always be honored as a Past Matron, the rest is all in fun!

☆　☆　☆　☆　☆

11. WHAT IS A PATRON?

Addendum Honoring Past Patrons

By FAY MAY, P.M. (*Ohio*)

(*Speaking parts for Worthy Matron and Star Points.*)

WORTHY MATRON:
We honor Past Patrons, the men in our lives, and pause to consider what these dedicated brothers mean to us.
Sister Adah, from the ray of blue,
Tell us what a Patron means to you.

ADAH:
A Patron exemplifies fidelity by always being on hand.
I admire his service and I think he's grand!

WORTHY MATRON:
Sister Ruth, tell us from the ray of yellow,
Do you consider a Patron a good fellow?

RUTH:
A Patron's constancy endures throughout the year;
Some Patrons have served more than once here.

WORTHY MATRON:
Sister Esther, from your ray of white,
Is a Patron a symbol of light?

ESTHER:
A Patron gives us light when he knows the work,
And the officers see the light and never shirk.

WORTHY MATRON:
Sister Martha, how is a Patron seen
From your vantage point of green?

MARTHA:
Faith and hope are a Patron's creed;
He gives us the confidence we need.

WORTHY MATRON:

Sister Electa, from the beautiful red ray,
What is your opinion of a Patron today?

ELECTA:

A Patron does his work with a fervency we share.
His interest is reflected in our chapter everywhere.

WORTHY MATRON:

We are grateful to our Masonic brothers for sharing their heritage with us, and especially to those who have been our leaders, our Past Patrons.

☆   ☆   ☆   ☆   ☆

12. ADDENDUM HONORING PAST MATRONS

By FAY MAY, P.M. (*Ohio*)

*Short speaking parts for W.M., Cond., Warder, A.M.,
A.P., A.C., and Star Points.*

CONDUCTRESS: P is for the pride with which you did preside.

WARDER: A is for your great ability.

A. MATRON: S for your success and sociability.

A. PATRON: T for truth, which has always been your guide.

A. COND.: M is for many meetings you've attended.

ADAH: A for ardor in all you do.

RUTH: T is for our trust in you.

ESTHER: R for the right you always defended.

MARTHA: O for oaths you took with care and lived to the letter.

ELECTA: N is for nice, which you are; in fact, you couldn't be better.

W. MATRON: We have spelled PAST MATRON, the title of respect and affection with which we love to greet you.

☆   ☆   ☆   ☆   ☆

13. A THOUGHT FOR PAST MATRONS NIGHT

By Cornelia Schatmeyer, P.M. (*New Jersey*)

(This may be given by one person, or by several as indicated by verses)

We'd like to leave a thought with you
About Past Matrons Night,
One to set you thinking
And put your thoughts aright.
Past Matrons who have served us well,
In chapters here and there,
Will always keep our ideals high
Because they really care.

This special night, we've set aside,
Holds a fraternal key
To unlock the doors of sisterhood,
And this should always be.

In honoring Past Matrons,
And Past Patrons, you will find
That we're bringing friendship to ourselves
That's of the better kind.

We are not islands to ourselves,
We need each others' love
Remembering the commandment
Of our Father up above.
So, in loving one another,
Our bonds of friendship weave,

CEREMONIES

Then, joining up in spirit,
We surely will perceive
That the good work of our Order
Is like a pleasant two-way street
Where sisters greet each other
Whenever they may meet.

Past Matrons represent a bond,
We're glad that they belong
And are proud of each and every one,
For they keep our Order strong.

☆　☆　☆　☆　☆

14. SHORT CEREMONY HONORING PAST MATRONS AND PAST PATRONS

By Dorothy Trimble, P.M. (*Indiana*)

Worthy Matron:

Sister Conductress, what would you say that you have to be thankful for today?

Conductress:

Worthy Matron, I would say that we have a lot to be thankful for. Our pioneer ancestors left us a wonderful heritage for somewhere down through the years they gave us our Eastern Star. Tonight, we can be thankful for the friends we have here who are Past Matrons and Past Patrons of our beautiful Order.

As Matrons and Patrons, they may be *past,* but their places in the Chapter will always *last.*

Worthy Matron:

Sisters Conductress and Associate Conductress, will you escort the Past Matrons and Past Patrons to the East.

(after they are in the East)

Grown-up folks don't always say
Thanks for favors sent their way,
But tonight we have not forgotten
So we'll just say "thanks a lot,"
Not only for the past, but the present
And we thank you for just being you.

(*Conductresses present each one with a small gift from the Chapter and then escort them back to their seats.*)

☆　　☆　　☆　　☆　　☆

15. CHRISTMAS

By Margaret Melissinos (*New York*)

Worthy Matron:
> Within the portals of this room
>> It's always Christmas Eve;
> Our lovely Star dispels the gloom
>> As we, in awe, perceive
> The warmth and brightness of its rays
>> That beckon us, "Come hither,
> And cast behind you weary days,
>> And cause your cares to wither."

Associate Matron:
> Our shepherds sit on every side
>> To guide us in the night;
> To set the pattern of our stride,
>> To keep our Star in sight.

Chaplain:
> To follow where its light may lead,
>> To show us if we stray
> That in its warmth we'll find, indeed,
>> That peace for which we pray.

Marshal:
> And as we follow in its beam,
>> Its lovely points reach down
> And touch our hearts, as it would see,
>> With tales of great renown.

Conductress:
> With stories woven with emotion,
>> Of love and charity,
> Of justice, courage and devotion,
>> Of faith and piety.
> With tale of trust and fortitude,

Of truth and constancy,
All morals of great magnitude
To guide us constantly.

ASSOCIATE CONDUCTRESS:

And when we come to Bethlehem,
Our weary journey ended,
That Truth, from which all joy may stem,
Awaits us, bright and splendid.

WORTHY MATRON:

And through His Son, our God will smile
And say, "Twice blessed you are
Because you followed, mile for mile,
My lovely Eastern Star."

☆　☆　☆　☆　☆

16. SITTIN' AND ROCKIN'
Ceremony to Honor Retiring Matron and Patron

By DOROTHY TRIMBLE, P.M. (*Indiana*)

ASSOCIATE MATRON:
Worthy Matron, with your permission, if I may,
There's something I would like to say.
Without your knowledge, we have planned
A little service—nothing grand,
But merely to end up with a flourish
A year whose memories you'll always cherish.

ASSOCIATE CONDUCTRESS:
No, we would never be so bold
As to suggest that you're growing old,
But being Matron and Patron has a way
Of ageing one from day to day,
Although there are remedies or, so I'm told,
To combat the process of growing old.

CONDUCTRESS:
I would recommend, by all means,
A spring tonic of good old dandelion greens
And a rocking chair that you sit in and rock,
And wriggle your toes, without shoes or socks.

(*There is a knock at the door*)

WARDER:
Worthy Matron, there is a knock at the door.
I'll see who it is, then we'll tell you more.

(*Two rocking chairs are brought in and placed in
the East*)

175

ASSOCIATE MATRON:

Sisters Conductress and Associate Conductress,
I think it is only fair
For our friends to try out these rocking chairs.
So, let the music sound, the trumpets blare,
As you escort them to their rocking chairs.

(*Music: "When You and I Were Young, Maggie"*)

PROMPTER:

Worthy Matron, Worthy Patron,
The cheapest thing, outside of rice,
That I can give you, is advice.
For years, to me, for advice you look
Because I dished it out from this little book.

MARSHAL:

Worthy Matron, Worthy Patron,
If you will allow me, I am sure
That as your Marshal, I can procure
Advice from every angle and point—
From Emily Post to aching joint.

ASSOCIATE PATRON:

Brother _____, my advice to you
To insure success in all you do,
Is just to sit there and rock away
And let the women have their say.

ADAH:

Worthy Matron, for any ache, or pain, or ill,
I would advise tranquilizer pills.
By my advice, you should be led
Or, like me, you might lose your head.

RUTH:

    Take my advice, and it's the truth—
    You'll never find a task like Ruth's.
    Instead of hunting grain to shock,
    Just sit in your rocking chair and rock.

ESTHER:

    Married or not, you can take my advice:
    Like Esther, be beautiful and nice,
    And if any argument you do not win,
    Instead of a crown, get a rolling pin.

MARTHA:

    When to your rocking chair you've took,
    I recommend the "best seller" book.
    And if your eyesight is only fair,
    Keep a pair of specs by your rocking chair.

ELECTA:

    A lady should be prim and nice
    And always hand out good advice.
    So, I'll just say, for old-times sake,
    Sometimes, let's have a coffee break.

CHAPLAIN:

    Advice from a Chaplain should be good as gold
    When you're sittin' and rockin' and growin' old,
    So, I'll just say a little prayer
    That you can still make it up the stair.

    *(Conductresses present each with miniature rocking
    chair and escort them back to their stations.)*

☆   ☆   ☆   ☆   ☆

17. CEREMONY TO HONOR RETIRING MATRON WHOSE HUSBAND IS PATRON

By Dorothy Trimble, P.M. (*Indiana*)

WORTHY MATRON ELECT:

Worthy Matron, may I approach the East?

WORTHY MATRON:

You may.

W. M. ELECT (to W. P.):

Worthy Patron, I am looking for something; will you held me find it?

WORTHY PATRON:

As Worthy Patron, it is my duty to help whenever I can. May I ask what you are looking for?

W. M. ELECT:

I am seeking the truth.

WORTHY PATRON:

The truth about what?

W. M. ELECT:

The truth about a girl named _____.

WORTHY PATRON:

Well, truth never changes, that's my _____. Since I'm the man that's married to _____, I may know more about _____ than most,

_____ may be merry, or _____ may be mad,

But a better wife no Mason or man ever had.

W. M. ELECT:

Sister Conductress, do you know the truth about _____?

CONDUCTRESS:

The name is common and very old,

Given to the gentle, and also the bold,

The better you know her, the better you love her,
She's like the cream in my coffee, the beef in my stew,
Know _____? you bet your sweet life I do!

W. M. ELECT:

Sister Associate Conductress, what did you say about
_____?

ASSOCIATE CONDUCTRESS:

What about _____? Well, I declare
I'm so glad you put me on the air.
She came here from the town of so-and-so,
(Their loss was our gain when they let her go)
From way up north, to way down thar,
We know, sure enough, that she's a Star.

W. M. ELECT:

Sisters Electa, Martha, Esther, Ruth, and Adah,
You are sworn to tell the truth,
So, tell me now, though your stories may vary,
Just where you heard the truth about _____.

ADAH:

I heard it by grapevine,

RUTH:

By telephone,

ESTHER:

Just chewing the fat,

MARTHA:

The twilight zone,

ELECTA:

I heard it at a coffee break

W. M. ELECT:

Then tell it to me for old-times sake.

ADAH:

She loves our Order, and children, too,

She likes a house with a western view,
The grapevine says she is kind and good.
If you don't know _____, I think you should.
RUTH·
She's a special good scout,
She enjoys a joke,
To help a friend, she'd go for broke.
When I listen in on the party line
The comments about her are mighty fine.
ESTHER:
The truth about _____, I could tell quite a few
For nobody talks any more than I do.
But I'm pressed for time, and what I can say
Would probably take me the rest of the day.
So, I'll just say one thing, and you all will agree—
She's been a wonderful friend to you and to me.
MARTHA:
I don't know her church, but I can recall
She always has a good word for them all;
She supports the Job's Daughters (*or Rainbow, etc.*)
    and the DeMolay
And all the worthwhile things that turn up her way.
Whatever the need of a friend may be,
She gives help, or cheer, or sympathy.
ELECTA:
The things I hear at my coffee break!
Yes. I'll tell them to you for old-times sake.
She loves her neighbors, likes good clean fun,
She's always just _____ with everyone.
No, truth never changes, though circumstances vary,
And you are lucky if you have a pal like _____.

☆　☆　☆　☆　☆

180

18. FATHERS DAY CEREMONY
For any Young Girls Group

By MARGARET MELISSINOS (*New York*)

Short speaking parts for twelve and Chaplain.

1ST SPEAKER:

Tonight is a very special night; we're saluting special
lads—

The most important men in our lives—our dear, and
grand old Dads.

Dear Chaplain, will you please offer a prayer at our
altar for all fathers everywhere?

CHAPLAIN (*approaches altar and kneels*):

Heavenly Father, please bestow a special blessing on
all fathers this night, and especially all fathers in this
room, for their patient guidance and dutiful devotion
to their families, for their indulgence with our short-
comings, and their untiring efforts to lead us in Thy
path. Please help us to be the daughters they would
have us be, that in the afternoon of their lives, they
may find contentment and satisfaction in a job well
done. For this we thank you, God. Amen. (*returns to
her floor position*)

2ND SPEAKER:

We're much too busy through the year to take the
time to say

How wonderful Dads are—how dear—and then comes
Fathers Day!

3RD SPEAKER:

We take Dad so for granted in our adolescent greed;

We beg, cajole, we rave, and rant for things we think
we need.

181

4TH SPEAKER:

We never seem to care enough; we really do, in truth;
But feelings do not lend themselves to easy words, in
youth.

5TH SPEAKER:

A parting kiss when we go out may seem to be in
haste,
But, Dad, its hidden meaning says you cannot be
replaced.

6TH SPEAKER:

We never seem to listen when you're giving us advice,
But, Dad, we get the message about ladies being nice.

7TH SPEAKER:

We always want another dress, another pair of shoes;
No matter how much we have, we always sing the
blues!

8TH SPEAKER:

And when we seem to fight you over mediocre things,
It's not really you we're fighting, we're just trying
out our wings.

9TH SPEAKER:

Then, suddenly, we realize a precious year has
passed—
There's added lines to Daddy's eyes—and time is fleeting fast.

10TH SPEAKER:

I guess, you'd say, we're very near the age of understanding—
The house will quiet down a bit, and we'll be less
demanding.

182

11TH SPEAKER:

We'll bring your pipe and slippers when your weary
day is through,

We'll help Mom with the dishes so she will not bother
you.

12TH SPEAKER:

We promise to be better girls—for each fault, we'll
atone—

But let us keep our *RECORDS*, and the *LOVELY
TELEPHONE!*

*(Optional girls pass out Fathers Day gifts, and
when they are finished, the SOLOIST sings to
the tune of "Mother"):*

SOLOIST:

F—is for our fathers, heaven bless them,

A—is for the strong arms always there,

T—is for the times that we outguess them,

H—is for what happens when we dare.

E—means that they're everything we cherish,

R—means when they're right, we think they're wrong,

Put them all together, they spell FATHER—the man
who's hero of our song.